In the Dark
with my Dress on Fire

In the Dark
with my Dress on Fire

My life in Cape Town, London, Havana and Home Again

Blanche La Guma
with Martin Klammer

First published by Jacana Media (Pty) Ltd in 2010

10 Orange Street
Sunnyside
Auckland Park 2092
South Africa
(+27 11) 628-3200
www.jacana.co.za

© Blanche La Guma and Martin Klammer, 2010

ISBN 978-1-77009-922-7

Cover design by Jacana Media

Set in Ehrhardt 11/14pt
Printed and bound by Ultra Litho (Pty) Ltd Johannesburg
Job No. 001319

See a complete list of Jacana titles at www.jacana.co.za

Preface

I should like to dedicate this book to my sons, Eugene and Barto, who steadfastly supported me despite the hardships they endured, and to my niece Carol Smith, Enid Heber, Amy Thornton and other friends who helped me recall some of the events of my life.

I should also like to thank my editor, Professor Martin Klammer, who encouraged me to write this book and did a vast amount of research to confirm and give shape to my story. This book would not have been written had it not been for his assistance.

Blanche La Guma
Cape Town
September 2010

Introduction

When I was newly married I worked as a nurse-midwife in the poorer communities of Cape Town and Athlone. The four maternity hospitals that served 'Non-Europeans' in the mid-1950s were so crowded that women who gave birth were sent home early to make room for others. Most of the time the hospitals took only the most complicated cases or women awaiting their first babies, leaving the rest of the deliveries to us midwives.

Many of the women couldn't afford the fee of £3 for ante-natal care, the delivery and ten days of post-natal care. They tried to pay in instalments – which they rarely completed – or didn't pay at all. We'd work for free and, if they wanted our services again, we'd return for second, third and fourth deliveries. We were dealing with human beings, after all.

One night I was called for the delivery of Mrs M in Rylands, at that time a poor area in Athlone. The home was a *pondokkie*, a shack connected to other shacks by mud roads. When I arrived just past eleven o'clock, Mrs M was lying on newspapers on a bed. The space was so small that she was unable to stretch out her legs. I squeezed myself in so that I could guide the baby out. The father stood nearby while four little toddlers crouched in a lean-to outside and waited, shivering in the cold until they could come back to see their newborn brother or sister.

The tin roof just overhead was leaking from a Cape storm. The room was lit only by two candles – one in front for me to see the baby coming through and one behind where I had placed my swabs.

I was using both hands to turn the head so it wouldn't tear the perineum as it came through. As the light was dim I did this mostly by feel. Just as the baby's head emerged, a gust of wind blew rainwater through the leaking roof down onto the candle in front, snuffing it out. Suddenly I was working almost completely in the dark.

During this point in the birth, once the head and neck are out, there are a few minutes of what we call restitution. When the head comes through, you immediately clear the mouth to let in air. But you also have to help the baby's shoulders turn. You release the first or anterior shoulder and then the posterior shoulder and bring the baby up over the mother's belly.

Just as I was ready to bring the rest of the baby through, I began to feel an intense heat on my bottom. The candle behind me had set my uniform on fire! I could feel I was burning a bit, but before I put out the flame, I had to finish the delivery. There I was – in the rain, in the dark, with my dress on fire – delivering a baby!

I then reached back with one hand and extinguished the flame while keeping my other hand on the baby's head. The mother realised what was going on and seemed quite pleased that I was concentrating on her. With the fire out, I completed the final delivery of the baby in the dark.

When I came home in the early hours of morning Alex was waiting up. Seeing the dirt and bloody mess on my uniform, he asked, 'What happened?' Then he saw my bottom. 'Blanche,' he said, 'you burnt your bottom!' He was that kind of guy – finding humour in many circumstances. 'Yes I did,' I said, 'and you're lucky to have me come home at all!'

He knew that in the work I did, this sort of thing could happen. Later, he used much of this story at the end of his novel, *And a Threefold Cord*.

○

Around this time I wrote an essay about the effect of the deplorable living conditions on mothers and infants. It was titled 'A Child is Born' and published in *New Age*, the journal for which Alex worked in Cape Town. I wrote that 'a whole book could be written' about the tragic stories observed by midwives all over South Africa. That a country that produced so much wealth 'should allow millions of mothers to bring their sons and daughters into the world in abject poverty and such awful conditions as I have seen, is, to say the least, a shocking disgrace and far out of standing with modern civilisation'. Yet I concluded on a note of hope that in the future 'the people will come into their own and mothers of our new citizens will bear them without fear of over-crowded hospitals, leaking *pondokkies*, and the poverty and disease which doom our children even before they are born'.

It's more than fifty years since I wrote that. South Africa today is not without its problems. There are still over-crowded hospitals, leaking *pondokkies*, poverty and disease. But with the demise of apartheid, we are beginning to light our way out of the darkness of the past.

I tell this story not to call attention to my own heroics, but to suggest that in the world in which I came of age many such extraordinary deeds were done by ordinary people and went unrecognised every day – indeed, even for lifetimes. While this book is about my life, it's also the story of the many people who walked with me on our long journey to freedom. It's the story of my loving mother who raised me from frail beginnings into the young woman I was to become. It's the story of the many people in Cape Town in the 1950s and 1960s who suffered detention, banning, and even torture to end apartheid. And it's the story of my loving husband, Alex, who was my partner in all things personal and political, and of our two sons, Eugene and Barto, who showed courage in trials beyond those which children should have to endure. It's the story of all those who stood by me – in Cape Town, London and Havana.

Though this is my account, I hope people will see it as part of the larger story of South Africa and of our freedom for which so many struggled and sacrificed, a story that is not yet finished, but that promises what I had hoped for more than fifty years ago – a future in which all of our people 'will come into their own'.

Blanche La Guma

Chapter 1

'We were poor, but we never felt poor'

I was born at home in the early hours of the morning of 30 November 1927 in Athlone, about seven miles as the crow flies from the centre of Cape Town. I arrived two months prematurely – a tiny 'shoebox baby'. I was the fifth and last child, one of two girls in the family of Peter and Sophia Herman.

At first my mother didn't even know she was in labour. After my birth the doctor who delivered me, Charles Shapiro, advised my mother to keep me warm. I was fed with a pipette, a thin tube attached to a small bottle slightly tilted to allow the milk to flow gently into my throat while my mother held me. Babies as small and weak as I was often died soon after birth. Yet I wasn't placed in an incubator or sent to hospital for special treatment. The doctor must have thought it wasn't worth the effort, since ambulance and hospital services would have been poor in Athlone, a suburb that was itself in its infancy.

Dr Shapiro did his best under the circumstances. He was the first doctor in Athlone, a kind and understanding Jewish man fulfilling an important humanitarian role for very poor people. When patients couldn't pay he didn't go after them, nor did he turn them down when they called on him again. My mother, in fact, was one of those who needed a long time to settle their bills.

⌒

Our family was of mixed ancestry. On my father's side the family name was Hermann, later anglicised to Herman. My mother's surname, Mocke, was Dutch. But behind the German and Dutch on both sides there is some degree of Khoisan in us, and so we are of mixed race. In South African racial terminology we are 'coloured'. To use that term is not to be racist, as in the days of apartheid when the entire system was built on racial classifications. I'm just facing the truth of who I am and where my family comes from.

Neither of my parents was Capetonian by birth. My mother, Sophia Elizabeth, was born in Kimberley in 1893, the youngest of five girls. Her father, Jacobus (Koos) Mocke, was of such fair complexion that he could pass for white. He even managed to slip into Victoria College, now Stellenbosch University, where he earned a bachelor's degree.* He was a carpenter and cabinet-maker, a very religious man who made church pulpits among other things. Before that he'd been a diamond prospector in Kimberley in the late 1800s, having trekked with my grandmother, Elizabeth Wales, from Beaufort West to Kimberley by oxwagon. When he died in 1906, my mother went to Johannesburg to live with one older sister and then another. Having both parents die when she was young must have been difficult, and living with a sister is not the same as growing up with a parent. In 1912 when she was 19, my mother fell pregnant and gave birth out of wedlock to my eldest brother, Herbert.

My father, Peter Cornelius Herman, was born in 1888 in Port Elizabeth, the seventh of ten children. He grew up in a harsh household ruled by his father, a minister in the Congregational Church. I never met the man, but from what my father said he sounded like a horrible chap, one of those authoritarian preachers whose children must do as they say. He walked with his Bible in front while his wife and children came tripping along behind. He was selfish and cruel, and he treated my father terribly. When my father was 12 or 13 a foal disappeared from among the many horses his father owned. To discipline my father whom he accused of losing the foal, my grandfather tied him down with his head between his legs – not just for an afternoon but for three days. As a result my father developed a deformity for the rest of his life. His back was bent

---

* Victoria College acquired university status and became Stellenbosch University in 1918, the same year the University of Cape Town was formally established.

so badly that a hump formed between his shoulders. His spinal column never straightened out and he always leaned forward a bit.

Though my father completed only four or five years of school, he could read and write and do sums. After the gold mines opened in Johannesburg, his family moved there and he got a job in Robinson Deep, one of the deepest mines in South Africa. Few people know that coloured men as well as blacks worked on the mines. Later, just before the First World War, my father took work on the farms in South West Africa (now Namibia) under the colonial Germans, who were very harsh. At one point he worked there with Jimmy La Guma, Alex's father.

My father met my mother in Johannesburg, in what circumstances I never knew. My mother had Herbert by that time and needed support, which my father was happy to provide, though his family treated her terribly. Because she had a child out of wedlock, they didn't think she was good enough for him – or for them. When he took her to meet them, they didn't even want to know her. And they certainly didn't want Herbert's surname to change from Mocke to Herman.

My father felt differently. He was extremely fond of my mother. From the first he treated Herbert as if he were his own child, taking him under his wing and giving him his surname. In fact, I think it was partly because Dad's family didn't approve of his marrying Mother that they left Jo'burg and came to Cape Town, where they were married in 1915 in St Mary's Anglican Church, Woodstock. He was 27, she was 22, and Herbert was 3.

They never told Herbert he was illegitimate. Everything was fine until much later when Herbert was grown up and ran into Auntie Marie on the street. She was a real nasty bit of work. I always thought of her as 'the Vixen'. She didn't visit us much, but when she did it was only to see my father. She'd ignore my mother, refusing even to acknowledge when my mother spoke. Auntie Marie also made nasty comments like, 'Are *all* these children Peter's?' Eventually my father asked her not to come around anymore, though she persisted. When Herbert met up with her, Auntie Marie asked, 'Which name do you go under?' He didn't know he was illegitimate, so he said his name of course was Herbert Herman. She told him no, it *wasn't*. Then the whole thing came out. But my parents were always good to Herbert.

○

My parents came looking for a better life in Cape Town where job opportunities for people of colour had always been slightly better than elsewhere. They lived in District Six in Sheppard Street, where my other siblings were born: an older sister, Ella, and older brothers Jim and George. I know that many people today who were forcibly removed from District Six in the 1960s and 1970s have fond memories of living there, but District Six in the 1920s and even later was frankly a slum which many people, including my parents, tried to leave. Nonetheless, the community spirit in District Six was always strong: people had a sense of belonging.

In the mid-1920s my parents moved to the Gleemoor area of Athlone where I was born. (My brothers, all born in District Six, called me 'Vlak aap' – Cape Flats little ape.) The city of Cape Town had begun a home ownership programme in Athlone to encourage coloured people to move out of the city into newly planned areas on the Cape Flats. It was really a segregation scheme disguised as a housing opportunity. I appreciate their sacrifice in buying a house on such little income.

The Cape Flats were swampy, low-lying, barren, and windswept. There were no roads, shops, or playing fields. When my parents moved into Gleemoor, my father called the area 'godforsaken'. The roads were like white chalk. All my clothes were coloured white as a result, especially when it rained. Friends who lived in Woodstock or Salt River would ask, 'Woon julle nog daar buite?' (Are you still living out there in the countryside?) My parents joined the Gleemoor Civic Association to demand that the City Council make improvements such as street lights, tarred roads, and pavements, as well as filling in the swamps, establishing public transport, and building schools. My parents' civic commitment would later become a model for me during our struggle against apartheid.

My father worked in the printing industry when work was hard to get and harder still to keep. Every time my father found a job, the firm would close down and he'd be out of work. Then came the Depression and the only money he made was delivering letters for the printers' union secretary, who paid him 'two-and-six' – two shillings and sixpence.

My father travelled back and forth to Cape Town on his bicycle, looking for work. Once when he found a job after being out of work for ages, the boss wanted him to do something that my father felt was beneath his dignity. I don't know what it was, but I remember him coming home. My mother was so pleased he'd got work that when she saw him arrive early, she said, 'What happened?'

'I chucked the job.'

'You know things are terrible, Peter,' she said. 'What happened?'

'I told the boss to put that job where the monkey puts his nuts!'

'But Peter,' she said, 'do you even *know* where the monkey puts his nuts?'

My father paused. 'I don't actually,' he said. 'But that's what they say!'

My father and mother had a good laugh about that. I learned something from him, which rubbed off on me. Rather lose your job and preserve your dignity than live for ever on your knees.

○

My mother worked as a domestic to augment my father's income, washing and ironing and cleaning houses for white women. Most of the white madams were terrible. They had plenty of money yet they paid only 'three-and-six' (three shillings and sixpence) for working from eight to six, cleaning ten rooms in a double-storey house. They'd think nothing of paying one shilling and ninepence for 'half' a day, which was eight to three, or a penny to wash a shirt or a skirt, six pairs of socks or six hankies, and threepence for a sheet. My mother brought some of the washing home, using her own soap. I could see how badly she was treated and I felt bitter, really bitter. It was by watching her struggle to make ends meet that I developed my attitude against the exploitation of one human being by another.

During school holidays when I was about eight or nine years old, my mother didn't know what to do with me, so she took me with her to work. I especially remember a Mrs Hudson in Rondebosch. When we got there she was sitting in her chair, leaning back with her legs apart and a fly on her forehead, looking terribly crude. She was drunk. 'Go away, fly!' she said. I almost died laughing.

'Don't you watch!' my mother said. 'Go play outside. I don't want you in here.' Everything about the woman was so different from what my mother taught us about dignity. I can still picture Mrs Hudson. She had all that money but no self-respect.

Later, when I was in my teens, I took the washing back to the madams' homes on my bicycle. One of the places I went to was in Pinelands where we had to enter by the back door. We never entered through the front door.

Once when my brother George took the washing, this woman's little boy named David was playing in the yard. The woman told George, 'Give this to Master David.'

'I only have one Master,' my brother told her, 'and that Master's upstairs [meaning God]. I will *never* call your son a master.'

The woman later told my mother, 'Don't you *ever* send that rude boy of yours again. He's got no manners. He doesn't know how to treat people.' All because he refused to call her child 'master'.

That was the attitude of whites. Many of these madams were British, including this woman, who would actually *boast* that she was a colonial. They had their own country, yet they came to South Africa and exploited our people. It was easy here; it was good living for whites. My father once told his British boss: 'South Africa is a place where the milk and honey flows and the sun always shines, and you come here to eat us up.' For that he lost his job.

○

We were poor, always struggling to make ends meet. Only now do I realise how poor we were. It was normal to have only one pair of tackies (shoes). They were of such poor quality that they lasted only two weeks from the way I used to run and play. (I'd go barefoot until I could get another pair on my father's next payday.) I had only one school uniform. After school I'd wash my blouse, hang it out to dry, and iron it to be ready the next morning. I had one dress for church. After I came home from church I'd put it aside, running around in my little petticoat before I'd put the dress back on for Sunday school in the afternoon. At Christmas I often didn't have a special dress like other girls, so I just wore the one dress I had.

I don't know how my mother managed, but she never complained. She learned to stretch the little money we had. We never went hungry. She could really stretch the stew by making a big pot so that we all had a serving with the vegetable. We never went into debt. 'If you can't buy anything with cash, then you can't have it,' my mother said. As long as we were looked after and cared for and had food to eat, we learned to understand that we just couldn't have the fanciest clothes. The financial struggle must have been tremendous, but it never occurred to me that we were poor. Morally my parents were so strong that they overcame their financial difficulties. We were poor, but we never *felt* poor.[*]

---

[*] Coloured and black poverty was the direct result of a labour system introduced in the 1920s designed to favour whites. Until that time coloured men in Cape Town had performed most unskilled labour and a good part of skilled labour. Jobs were less divided along colour lines in Cape Town than anywhere else in South Africa. However, in the 1920s the government of J.B.M. Hertzog introduced a 'civilised labour policy' through laws that provided enormous advantages for white ('civilised') workers that today would be seen as an aggressive form of affirmative action.

Chapter 2

'I loved being the little girl doing all those fancy tricks'

I was terribly anaemic as a child. I had to take a strong iron tonic called
Parrish's Food in cod liver oil for many years. Every week I'd go with
my mother to the clinic to get a little bottle, which I had to shake up
before drinking. I had bottles and bottles of it as a child. I didn't like it
but I got used to it. My mother also gave me a soft-boiled egg each day
from the chickens she kept. Because I was so thin and delicately built,
I often played the fairy in school concerts. When I was about eight I
stopped taking the tonic, but my mother remained protective of me well
into my teens, always concerned I'd become ill.

As I grew older I began to enjoy outdoor activities and sport. My
mother encouraged me to exercise to grow into a strong, healthy child
because I'd been so weak when I was younger. When I was about 11 she
bought me a bike. I could hardly believe it. There was always something
I wanted but couldn't have, like a nice dress, because we just didn't have
money. By that stage my mother must have decided she would get me
the one thing I wanted so much, thinking I'd be more independent and
get out and play if I had a bicycle. I remember it cost £8. That was a
real sacrifice because we had no money. But I carried on so much about
having a bike that she bought it on credit, something unheard of in our
household. For a while she was able to pay the small monthly amount, but
when she couldn't keep it up, they came to fetch the bicycle. Everything
she had paid was lost. I was in tears. That bike was my only means of
getting around, my real friend.

When I was about 12, my brother George's friend started coming to our house with his bicycle on Sundays, and I took advantage of the opportunity. The friend's bike was what we called a 'fix' at that time. It had thin wheels and drop handles – a racer bike. It just *flew*.

As my brother and his friend would lie around and sleep all afternoon, I'd ask, 'Can I go for a spin around the block?' Then I'd take the bike and ride off. Once I'd left, nobody knew where I went. I didn't even know where I was going. I kept on the main road, all the way to Somerset West or Simon's Town. There were cars all the time going from Athlone towards Strand and Gordon's Bay, or in the other direction to Muizenberg or Kalk Bay. I didn't mind – I felt safe and on my own.

I really enjoyed those Sunday afternoons. I'd stop at the beach and swim or else cruise along with my thoughts, content with the bike just taking me where it would, and stop along the road to watch the vegetable growers and enjoy the peace and tranquillity of it all. When I got to Somerset West it didn't seem like I had ridden over 40 kilometres. I'd come back before sunset during our long summer twilight. When I walked in George's friend would say, 'The block has got very big, hasn't it?'

○

When I was about 10 or 11 my mother and I used to take the train into Cape Town on Sunday night to hear the municipal orchestra play at the City Hall under the direction of William J. Pickerill. At that time mainly whites attended, but there were also coloureds in the audience and we could sit anywhere.[*] My mother was clearly trying to teach me to appreciate classical music. Though we didn't have musical instruments at home, we did have a gramophone. The concerts gave me a much better understanding of what classical music was supposed to sound like. I enjoyed watching the different instruments and movements of the players. All the performers, of course, were white. Subsequently we also went to hear concerts by the Spes Bona Orchestra, an all-coloured orchestra with a coloured director, Dan Ulster, which performed in

---

[*] Formed in 1914, the Cape Town Municipal Orchestra played to both whites and coloureds, including working-class coloureds in District Six. Dr William J. Pickerill directed the orchestra from 1926 until 1947.

Gleemoor Town Hall in Athlone. These concerts always filled the hall with about 500 people attending.

When I was 11, my mother enrolled me in classes offered by the Eoan Group. The Eoan Group was a cultural organisation started in 1933 by an Englishwoman, Mrs Helen Southern-Holt, and her daughter Maisie.* Mrs Southern-Holt had been a ballet dancer in her earlier years, I believe, and Maisie was then a medical student and ballet dancer. The general goal was to help you become a more refined person. The Eoan Group taught movement, ballet and elocution to coloured children. All of our teachers were white. My mother wanted me to be able to speak correctly, behave correctly, and not become coarse.

I joined the Group when my school in Athlone arranged for girls to attend a fête in Cape Town at the Drill Hall. I don't think we girls were told that the sponsors of the event were Mrs Southern-Holt, Maisie and the renowned principal of the University of Cape Town Ballet School, Dulcie Howes. We were told to walk around the hall in a circle while being observed by the ballet teachers. A number of children were taken out and placed in the centre, and I was among them. This meant we had been accepted into the Eoan Group. And so I became a 'Grouper'.

Every Saturday I travelled by bus and train to St Paul's Hall in upper Cape Town and later Zonnebloem Hall in District Six to learn 'natural movements', which were loosening-up exercises in preparation for ballet at a later stage, and acrobatics. I loved it. I would show off to friends and family all the movements I was learning, even walking across the street on my hands. My mother couldn't stop me. By the time she saw what I was doing, I was already in the middle of the road.

Since I was very delicate and thin, I saw myself as a future ballet dancer. We learned 'operatic' in ballet movement, which is the beginning grade of ballet training, and also did barre work. When I was 12, I took part in my first and only ballet, *Scheherazade*. We performed at the City

---

* Mrs Helen Southern-Holt had been working with civic groups in District Six since 1926. She named the group Eoan, from the Greek word '*eos*' (meaning 'the Dawn'), based on the hope that the organisation would bring about a cultural dawning for coloured people. During the apartheid era, the Eoan Group was forced to move out of District Six under the Group Areas Act.

Hall before an audience of our parents plus others who supported the Eoan Group. I loved being the little girl doing all those fancy tricks, thinking that I really *was* a fairy.

I also went to elocution classes. We learned to speak English correctly, although my mother had already started training me before I joined the Eoan Group. We were also taught not to use coarse language and not to hang our head and shoulders while walking in the road. We had to walk upright. My mother played a key role in teaching me behaviour, personal hygiene, and correct speech. For her there was a right way to do things. And so despite the insecurity of my earlier years, with my mother's help I grew in confidence.

Sometimes I'd go to the Friendly Hall in Wale Street for midweek dance classes. We learned Spanish dances, the Irish jig, and Scottish dances like the Highland fling and the sword dance. Though the Eoan classes were free, each family had to buy their daughter a cream-coloured tusser silk tunic with a red sash and red 'Eoan' badge, which was worn during performances.

Blanche with her mother in Cape Town, 1939

When I started attending Trafalgar High School I couldn't cope with ballet practice as well as all of my homework. So of course I concentrated more on what I liked – the Eoan work – and my schoolwork suffered. I failed exams. Many of the Eoan girls had a similar problem. In the end I stopped going to Eoan Group for the simple reason that I couldn't do both my schoolwork and an hour's practice every day.

My mother had also told me there wasn't a chance of a coloured girl getting a top ballet position. Members of our group couldn't even qualify to be ballet dancers in South Africa. They had to go to England to sit their exams and qualify. We had two girls who actually did this. Both had been with the Group a long time, and when they performed together one of them danced the female role and the other the male role because there were no males in the Group. When it came time for these girls to do their qualifying exams, the Eoan Group held fundraising concerts and ballets to send them to England. Each girl passed with excellent results, earned the necessary certificate, and returned to South Africa. One of the girls was a few shades lighter than the other and could pass for white. She joined a white ballet school in Johannesburg, where it was easier to pass for white than in Cape Town.

In hindsight I realise that while the Eoan Group did good work, it also built up an elitist group in the coloured community. There weren't black members, and very few coloured parents could afford to let their children join. Parents would struggle and take on extra work just to afford the tusser silk tunics in addition to the child's school clothes. Everything those days came at a heavy price.

Chapter 3

'They were lucky if they got a bicycle and a suit'

In 1939, when I was 12, the United Party government under General Smuts joined the Allied forces in the Second World War. My father and my two brothers volunteered. They were patriotic, but they also hoped that by fighting for our country the system of segregation would change. My Dad was especially patriotic. When George and I criticised the government's segregation policy during the war, my Dad scolded us, calling us 'fifth columnists'. He told us about the greater threat of living under Nazism. (We didn't yet know about the Holocaust.) Having served in the First World War, my father was already 51 when the Second World War started – far too old to be in the field. When he registered he met one of the officers who had been with him in the First World War. He told my father he was over the age limit, which I think was 45. My father said, 'Well, I'm 45 and a little over!' They took him in and he did administrative work throughout the war in Johannesburg.*

My brothers, Herbert and James, joined the Cape Coloured Corps, a segregated unit that had been established during the First World War. Coloured men were employed as drivers and did other non-combatant work. The whites were afraid to give them guns because they feared they'd turn on them. Later the Indian-Malay Corps was formed separately, in

---

* South Africa's contribution to the war consisted mainly of supplying troops, men and material for the North African and Italian campaigns. Coloured opinion about the war was deeply divided. Coloured leaders, such as Cissie Gool of the Non-European United Front, initially denounced South Africa's participation, stating that the struggle for democratic rights at home was a higher priority. By June 1941, when German troops crossed the Soviet frontier, coloured leaders reversed course and supported the war.

part, I think, because of the Muslim observance of eating only halaal food. Black and coloured soldiers earned much less than whites and could not be promoted beyond the rank of sergeant-major. Even the highest-ranking officer in the Cape Corps or the Indian-Malay Corps had no authority over a white private and was paid less. I imagine black soldiers were treated even less well than the coloureds.[*]

My brothers went up to Libya where the Germans under General Rommel came sweeping across North Africa and captured Tobruk in 1942. At the fall of Tobruk, thousands of Allied soldiers were taken as prisoners of war, including my brothers.[†]

While my brothers and father were away, we often listened to news of the war on BBC radio, but we mainly followed events in the *Cape Argus*. I remember at one stage the Germans were sinking huge Allied convoys with their U-boats before the Allies were able to put a stop to it. Sometimes enormous Allied ships and aircraft carriers, mainly British, came to Cape Town harbour where we would go down and see them. Because of the fear of German spies, one of the slogans at the time was 'Don't talk about ships or shipping!'

Sirens kept us on the alert for the enemy. When you heard the siren it meant Cape Town was under a blackout. You had to black out your whole house and use only candles and black curtains so that no light shone through. People in the neighborhood were vigilant if someone lit a candle in the window. Smoking or lighting of cigarettes was also not allowed. When the siren sounded my mother, brother, and I made our way to Gleemoor Town Hall. Though it was pitch dark walking through those streets, I wasn't afraid. My mother was with me and somehow I thought she could conquer the world. She was part of a brigade that was supposed to make its way to the practice hall, though the others rarely

---

[*]   As in the First World War, only white troops were allowed to join combat units. Coloured, black and Indian soldiers enlisted in segregated corps and were confined to non-combatant duties as drivers, mechanics, builders, carpenters, typists, stretcher-bearers, cooks and even entertainers. In addition to the Cape Coloured Corps, the Native Military Corps and the Indian-Malay Corps supplied men for the war effort.

[†]   Tobruk was a strategically important seaport city in Libya, at that time a colony of Italy. When General Erwin Rommel's Afrika Korps conquered Tobruk on 21 June 1942, more than 35,000 British troops, including 11,000 South Africans, were taken prisoner.

turned up. I was amazed that on some occasions *nobody* was there – only us and my mother. Other people just couldn't see the seriousness of the situation. But we were disciplined and ready in case of an emergency. Whenever we heard the siren we'd go down to the hall, and when the siren sounded again and the lights came up, we'd return home, sometimes at two or three in the morning.

My mother was active in the local home defence, and so my brother and I sat and waited in the hall, cracking jokes about the fun of being in the dark. Sometimes we'd have a mock first-aid practice and my mother would bandage the legs of a 'victim' brought in on a stretcher. She also belonged to various charities that ran fundraisers for the war effort, especially concerts and dances for British and Australian soldiers in Cape Town.* My brother and I went along and I learned to dance the waltz, the quickstep and foxtrot, with my brother as my partner. Even though George was 17 and I was only 12, he was nice about it. He was protective of me because I was so very delicate. In any case, he was too shy to ask another girl for a dance.

Since this all happened before the Immorality Act – the 1950 apartheid law that prohibited sexual relations between persons of different races – many British and Australian soldiers met coloured or black girls at the dances, fell in love, took them home after the war and married them. It was openly known that the girls were going out with these guys, dancing together and holding hands in the street.

I occasionally danced with white soldiers when I got a little older, though none of them took an interest in me. I'd dance as long as my partner could do the quickstep. I just wasn't interested in boys. I was young and not very sophisticated. I was more interested in sport – hockey, netball and cycling. Only later did I start thinking seriously about boys, and even when a few fellows tried to become my boyfriend I really couldn't give a toss. Alex was my first serious boyfriend, and by then I was in my twenties.

---

* Women's organisations coordinated entertainment for soldiers during the war. Since coloured and black women were excluded from the South African Women's Auxiliary Services (SAWAS), they established their own organisations for coloured and black soldiers, including those from visiting transports.

O

During the war food was scarce, especially meat. At times we even ate whale meat, which was foamy while cooking. At the end of the war the government began food rationing. Huge military vans loaded with food would arrive at certain points – Gleemoor Town Hall, for instance – with sugar, rice, tea, butter and other staples. You never knew what was coming, but you took whatever came because you needed it badly.

My mother said we had to eat whatever she put on the table; we either ate or went without. Only people with stomach problems, like ulcers, were allowed to have white bread; everyone else had bread heavy with bran. A new industry developed out of this. Somebody got the idea to use a sieve with handles to sift the flour and extract the bran, leaving the white flour. At that time people didn't know the value of brown bread. There was a stigma attached to it because people thought that only poor people ate brown bread.

John Morley, a communist better known as Comrade John, initiated the Women's Food Committee (WFC) in Cape Town to oversee the distribution of food and organise queues so that people could get their food without squabbles or fights.* Like other communists, Comrade John had enlisted in 1941 when the Soviet Union joined the war on the side of the Allies. He was noted for driving his jeep through the camps, proudly flying a red flag on the bonnet in tribute to the USSR.

The Women's Food Committee was a mix of coloured and white activists that included my mother; Pauline Podbrey, a noted communist activist; and Katie White, a domestic worker from Claremont, who went on to become a leader of the Federation of South African Women (Fedsaw) in Cape Town.

The government didn't know how many people needed food, so they just filled the vans and those who queued early enough received their ration and those who came later missed out. Once a week George and I would arrive at ten o'clock at night at the collection point with our

---

* Food shortages plagued Cape Town during and after the war. In February 1945, Cape Town housewives marched on Parliament to demand food rationing. The Women's Food Committee (WFC), formed in late 1945, organised queues and distributed food to 30,000 predominantly coloured and black women at 45 distribution points.

sleeping bags, flask of tea and sandwiches so that we didn't miss our chance, but often a long queue had already formed. We'd sleep under the night sky while my mother moved up and down the line, making sure people were not cheating by trying to squeeze in dishonestly. She and the other women chatted most of the time and kept an eye on the children.

Even though my mother was committee chief for our area, we often got less than others because of her generosity. For example, George and I would each be allowed one two-pound packet of rice. But there was always someone with little children who couldn't all queue, so my mother would give more rice to them and less to us. We must never think only of ourselves, she'd tell us. 'You can do with a little less rice on your plate. Give it to that child there. You won't die. Take just enough to keep body and soul together.'

My mother was serious about any task she was given. She knew everybody and was looked up to because of her volunteer work in the community. She belonged to the St John Ambulance Brigade and performed first-aid and home nursing – she was really almost a paramedic. When the war was over, she'd go to the football field on Saturdays and do a stint as a first-aid nurse, bandaging injured footballers or rugby players. That was her strength: working for the community. Some of it rubbed off on me. Many times later in my life I'd think, 'I must do that because it's what Mommy would have done.'

○

After the war my brothers didn't want to speak about what happened up in North Africa. Jim was badly affected by shellshock – what's now called post-traumatic stress disorder. When the men were out in the Sahara Desert and hyenas came through the camp at night, Jim would go into a fit, howling and laughing. When he came home he did the same. Jim also suffered from chest trouble and repeated bouts of malaria caused by mosquito bites he got in tropical Africa. He eventually held down a job as a driver, but he never completely recovered. He was always doing strange things – contorting his face, acting like a hyena, pretending to drive a truck by turning an imaginary wheel, making engine sounds while pushing the gears and brakes, and imitating the sound of gunfire.

When white soldiers came home from the war, they were well compensated with houses, cars, money and good jobs. The Cape Corps and the Indian–Malay Corps veterans, on the other hand, were lucky if they got a bicycle and a suit.*

There was no money for a homecoming party for my father and two brothers. But we were just glad to have the family together again. I was so proud of my father and brothers. I secretly felt that the war hadn't reached South Africa and especially beautiful Cape Town because they had protected us.

Blanche with her father, then on active service, 1942

---

*   Official government policy stated that 'ex-servicemen should not suffer hardship after their discharge'. Yet black and coloured ex-servicemen suffered delays in pensions, gross underpayment in comparison to whites, and difficulty finding employment. In fact, the government's scheme of veterans' benefits was specifically designed on a racial basis.

Chapter 4

'Brother was separated from sister and families were broken up'

When I was growing up there were only two coloured high schools in Cape Town at the time – Trafalgar High in District Six, which I attended, and Livingstone High in Claremont. After completing my junior certificate (Grade 10 exam), I left school at the age of 16, much to the disappointment of my parents. I had done badly in the mid-year exams and just scraped through the finals. I knew I was wasting my time, especially in the light of how difficult it was for my parents to pay my school fees, books and train fares. Few coloured students finished Grade 12 as a result of financial stress.* I had the conscience to realise that my parents were struggling like blazes to keep me on a school bench when what I should do be doing was earning something to help out at home.

The only two professions open to coloured girls at the time were teaching and nursing. The year after I left Trafalgar High I started a two-year teacher-training course at Wesley Training College in Salt River. I dropped out after the first year, having failed hopelessly. For my 'pupil teaching' I was given a class of 60 sub-As (first-year pupils). That's 60 six- and seven-year-olds, each one different, each with his or her own needs, some of them unruly, and all of them needing to be controlled. I just couldn't cope. Every day I came home almost torn apart.

I also didn't have the clothes to look like a teacher. My school uniform, a black tunic and white blouse called a gym, was almost worn through on the right side where my briefcase rubbed against it. Things were so tough

---

*   Most coloured students at the time left school before even finishing the primary grades.

for my family that my parents couldn't afford to buy a new tunic. I darned and re-darned it so often that it was practically rewoven. When I stood in front of the class, the kids laughed at me. I felt like an outcast among my own friends who were better-off. It felt awful. I was at that age, 17 or 18, when things like this affected me badly. In fact, I was so poor I had to hide on the train just to get to school because I couldn't afford a ticket. Being a teacher was not for me. My parents were of course disappointed. They had hoped their little girl would go into teaching, because teachers had a high status in the community. 'My son is a teacher, you know!' It was a class distinction – the fact that you would be 'better' than a factory worker or an unskilled worker like my father. Though my parents tried to persuade me to stay in teaching, I wasn't going any further. When my mother realised this, she told me, 'You're not going to lie around at home. If you don't want to go to school, go out and work.'

There weren't any openings I was interested in, except becoming a nurse. But I could only take up midwifery nursing when I was 21. So I went to work in a cigarette factory in Observatory. I didn't work on the factory floor where they made the cigarettes but in the workers' canteen. Along with other girls I prepared vegetables and served food.

I'd heard a lot about factory life, and here I was seeing what it was like. Some of the girls in the factories were really rough. They'd get into horrible arguments, use vile language, and even fight. In fact, I left the factory because of a fight between the head cook, Mrs J, and one of the coloured girls who lived in Simon's Town near the naval base. She was a real sailor's girl, and if you went out with sailors you were thought to be rather loose. One day the cook just beat up this girl. She concocted a lie and said the girl was having an affair with her husband, just to give her an excuse to beat her. I've never seen two women fight like that. The girl's face was badly bruised and swollen from all the punches, though there was no blood. Though there were eight or ten of us working in the kitchen, nobody dared intervene. I saw the beginning of the fight, but walked away. I was afraid Mrs J would hit *me*.

Quite soon I could see I had no future at the factory. Mrs J, who had no schooling or manners, used to boast, 'I'm earning *top* wages!'

I said to her, 'Mrs J, how much is top wages?'

'Five bloody pounds!'

She'd been there twenty years. I thought to myself, 'Top wages at five pounds. I'm getting out.' My mother was pleased when I told her I was leaving; she thought that was best for me. I gave my week's notice and was gone. I had worked at the factory for about two years.

○

Before my marriage to Alex I took life free and easy. I joined an amateur hockey club in Athlone that competed against other coloured teams from Wynberg, Mowbray and Cape Town. Because I was a sprinter, I played wing or centre forward. Though I wasn't a particularly good player, I enjoyed running up and down the field.

Some of the girls in the team were teachers, like my friend Millie Gunn. We practised on Saturdays at St Raphael's Catholic school in Athlone and travelled to away matches by bus. In addition to hockey, softball clubs for women and baseball clubs for men were popular in the coloured communities. In fact, Alex played for a baseball team called the Comets.

After the hockey matches our team would go to a party at somebody's house or to the town hall where a dance was being held. Four or five chaps who used to cheer us on at hockey matches would go with us. They were just friends, though; no hanky-panky. They called us a lot of mad girls because we always had a real good time.

I learned the folk dance called 'the square', which was especially popular at the time. A leader – usually a man – would lead a square of four couples. The first dance was called the quadrille, the second a commercial, and the third a commercial quadrille. In each set you'd dance and intermingle and then come back. At the end you had to be back with your right partner, in your right place, and in your right square. It was complicated. Nobody would leave the hall until the band had played all three squares.

I used to have a lovely time dancing the squares and letting off a lot of energy. If the hall was a long way from Athlone, where most of us lived, we'd go by car – really a convoy of cars, because two squares meant sixteen people. In addition to the squares, we also danced the waltz and the quickstep jive, which was popular at the time.

But I then began having trouble with my mother. She was usually soft and gentle like my father. But as I grew older I began to defy her. One night she told me I had to be home at twelve o'clock. But the first square only started at ten and the whole square was quite long. In addition, there were other dances between the squares. Of course I couldn't leave until I'd finished *all* the squares.

It was about one o'clock when I started to make my way home by train. The last train at one or two o'clock was called the caboose, and at the end of the night we'd all rush to catch it. Quite often if we missed the last train or bus we'd walk home to Athlone from Wynberg or even from Cape Town, about seven miles. We were a bunch of mad girls together – Millie, Cookie, Gilda, Lorraine, Angela, and me, all part of our hockey team – singing, walking, dancing, performing on the streets, just having fun. And the summer nights were beautiful – warm and clear, with the moon over Table Mountain. By the time we got home it was usually one or two o'clock, even later.

'Where have you been?' my mother asked when I came home late one night. Then she began to beat me with a cane. I was 19 years old and still working in the cigarette factory. She'd never had a girl that age defy her, and she didn't know how to handle the situation. With each beating I only became more defiant. One or two weeks later I'd go off to a party again and come in late. I suppose it was my own 'Defiance Campaign'.

Looking back, I realise her great fear was that I'd come home pregnant. She herself had had a child before marriage and was hurt as a result, as had my sister Ella. As I grew older she probably thought she was protecting me as a young woman because of what had happened to her. She was open with me about sex; she didn't mince words. She told me exactly how the sex act works. 'Don't come and tell me you didn't know because I didn't put it to you clearly,' she'd say. But she couldn't understand I wasn't going in that direction at all. I just wasn't interested in boys. After a while she realised that beatings didn't work, and gave up.

I had won. I still went to dances and parties. And why not? I was having a good time.

O

Before the restrictions of apartheid came down on us, my friends and I went to all the best beaches. At Christmas time people camped all along the coast – Hout Bay, Buffels Bay, Froggy Pond, any number of places. One Christmas my friends and I went for three days to a lovely spot in Hout Bay called Paradise Grove. It was a camp with a large dance-floor. We would dance through the night into the early hours of the morning. That's where I did my best jitterbugging. Depending on how hot it was, we'd sleep in a tent or right outside, lying in the open and looking up at the most beautiful southern night sky.

*Blanche outside her parents'
home in Gleemoor, 1948*

○

In 1948, just before I turned 21, the National Party came to power. The Nats (as we called them) won on what they called their mandate – the promise of job reservation for whites – and once they got into power they began to fulfil this mandate by placing white Afrikaners in the civil service. 'Poor whites' from rural areas were put in charge of coloured men, who were fairly sophisticated city men on the whole, or else took their jobs. They spoke only Afrikaans, while Capetonians at the time spoke mainly English.

We foresaw a bleak future. The Population Registration Act of 1950 classified people in racial groups according to skin colour and supposed 'racial' features. It was a vicious piece of legislation. People whose 'race' was in question had to go to the municipal offices to be assessed and find out whether they were white, coloured, Indian or black African. You were judged by your facial features, your hair, and whether you had an aquiline or a flat-bridged nose. The authorities would push a pencil through your hair. If the pencil didn't slide smoothly through because your hair was woolly, you might be classified as coloured or as black African. Fortunately, I never had to be classified.

The coloured community is a mixed-race people. Some are quite dark in complexion, some are brown, while others are quite fair and could, as the term goes, 'pass for white'. In a number of families some of the children were 'white' and others dark. The brother might have thick woolly hair and, if the pen stuck there, he'd be reclassified as coloured or black. Though his sister also had kinky hair, the pen might trail through and she'd become white. Thus brother was separated from sister and families were broken up.

If you were white or could pass for white, you had a better chance in life – getting a job and earning more, having more freedom socially, and being recognised as white by other whites. Some fairer coloured people even tinted their hair to help them 'become' white. In the same way, some lighter-skinned blacks were classified as coloured. Because of this system of racial classification, a few parents even abandoned their darker children. Little ones might be placed in a crèche or given to somebody to keep for a while. Those in the family classified as white would then move to a white Group Area without returning to fetch the children. We read in the paper and heard about many sad cases of young people who later committed suicide.

When close friends passed each other in the street, the one who'd opted for white would ignore his or her darker friends. The fair one would go to a white school and the black one to the black school. Job offers in the newspapers would read, 'Slightly coloured needed as a typist.' If you felt you were 'slightly coloured' you'd apply. But if the boss felt you were not white enough, you were told you were too black. The situation disorientated people. I still meet people every day who do not know what or who they are.

What a false scam apartheid was! With the passage of the Prohibition of Mixed Marriages Act, a couple already legally married couldn't live together anymore if the husband was white and the wife was coloured. Marriages were broken up. Some interracial couples left the country and got married in another country, but then could not return to South Africa. And what about the children? Born of the same parents, some were fair and some dark. They grew up and played together. But eventually the white one would no longer be the black one's brother. How could the Nats play with lives like that? They ruined families and family life. It's terrible to think about, even now.

The Immorality Act went even further and made sexual relations between individuals from different groups illegal. Funnily enough, some of the main culprits were dominees of the Dutch Reformed Church. The sentencing in these cases was entirely unequal. The black girl would go to prison for nine months, while the white man usually got off with a suspended sentence from the judge – often, like him, an Afrikaner.

○

Like all these laws, the Group Areas Act (1950) brought terrible suffering. District Six in Cape Town stands out as the prime example of the application of this law, which forced people to live in segregated areas based on their 'racial' classification. Alex was born and raised in

District Six, a colourful, vibrant part of the city, even though much of it was a slum. Alex loved his district and his first novel, *A Walk in the Night*, provides a sense of what life there was like. But the apartheid regime's intention was to clear the city of blacks, including coloureds, and send them to outlying areas, breaking up close-knit communities. People were moved to the Cape Flats where new townships were established like Hanover Park and Mitchell's Plain, miles from the city and from work. The so-called flatlets provided here were really more like barracks, a place where gangsterism thrived.

I shudder at the thought of the past under apartheid. Once in the late 1950s when Alex and I were living in Athlone, there was an accident just outside on the corner. A white man had been hit by a car and was bleeding heavily. I wanted to give him aid, but he was badly injured and I was worried about making a wrong move and damaging his neck or vertebrae. When the ambulance arrived I thought, 'Oh no, they have sent a black ambulance' – that is, an ambulance that could carry only black patients. The driver had to turn back because if he took the man he'd be punished for breaking the law. I then ran home to call a second ambulance. The 'white' ambulance arrived in another half-hour, but by this time the injured man had died.

This is the kind of thing that happened under apartheid. A system built by whites and for whites killed a white man. One more thing: the two ambulances weren't even going to different hospitals, but to different parts of the *same* hospital! There was a black side and a white side to Groote Schuur. Ridiculous, but true. And when a black baby was born prematurely and incubators stood empty on the white side, they couldn't use one of them to save the life of the black baby. That baby either survived or died on its own.

Chapter 5

I became a member of the Communist Party in the late 1940s when I was in my early twenties. I knew a few communists from the time they visited our house to recruit my mother. Pauline Podbrey and Fred Carneson would come for tea on Saturdays and try to get Mother to join because they knew she had worked for Communist Party candidates in City Council elections, such as Alex's father James La Guma, Betty (Radford) Sachs, and Sam Kahn. Pauline and Fred would have recruited my father, too, but he was always out watching football or rugby.

Though my mother always supported the Communist Party, she didn't want her name on their books in case the information some day fell into the hands of the Nationalist government. When the Nats came to power, they banned the Communist Party. My mother felt that if she was arrested she might not be strong enough to refuse to divulge names and would end up betraying comrades. So when Pauline and Fred came around, she said, 'Look, I will work for you, I will go and canvass for Sam Kahn, but I can't join. I don't want my name there. The first people arrested will be the communists.' She felt she couldn't take the pressure. I take my hat off to her: she was honest.

Sam Kahn was a stalwart leader and a real inspiration to us. My earliest involvement with the Communist Party came when working alongside my mother on his 1943 election campaign. At that time blacks and coloureds could not represent themselves in Parliament but were represented by whites. Since Sam Kahn ran as the 'Native

Representative' of black Africans, my mother couldn't actually vote for
him, but we campaigned for him in Langa and other townships. He was
the first communist elected to Parliament in 1948. The people realised
the only person they could rely on was a member of the Communist
Party. Sam Kahn spoke out fearlessly against apartheid and in favour of
the people who elected him. I remember one election when the booths
were supposed to be open till seven o'clock, but at five to seven they
started to close the doors of the Athlone municipal hall. Sam Kahn went
in, a big hefty man, and as they tried to shut the doors he got in the
middle and pushed them open from the other side so the people could go
in to vote. He knew that every vote counted. He was a real character, and
he got on with everybody, too. He was only allowed to stay in Parliament
for a short time before he was banned as a communist and had to give
up his seat.*

○

I was about 17 or 18 when I first tried to join a branch of the Communist
Party in Athlone formed by Jack Tarshish. Quite a few of us young
people joined though the branch closed after a short time. Later I began
attending evening lectures by Party members. After a day of working in
the cigarette factory I'd go straight to meetings in Queen Victoria Street
in town. Mostly young people attended the lectures. We learned what it
meant to be a communist and what we were going in for. My lecturer on
Tuesday nights was Chek Chekonovsky – I never knew his first name –
and on Thursdays it was Ike Horvitch.† Many of these communists were
Jews whose parents had emigrated from Russia and especially Lithuania.
From the very first years of apartheid they stood by us.

When I came home from classes on communism I didn't feel I could
tell my mother where I had been. When I started coming home late
on Tuesdays and Thursdays I knew my mother might object because

---

*   Sam Kahn, a young Jewish lawyer and Communist Party activist, was voted into Parliament
     in 1948 by black African voters in the Western Cape, then banned in 1950 and unseated
     from Parliament in 1952 under the Suppression of Communism Act. Kahn was known in
     Parliament for his acerbic wit and sharp condemnation of apartheid policies.
†   Isaac O. 'Ike' Horvitch became national chairman of the CPSA in 1949. He was one of 156
     tried for treason in the Treason Trial (1956-1961).

she was afraid that if I became a communist I'd be arrested and suffer consequences too terrible to mention. So I just didn't say anything. Even the books I read I had to hide.

Once when I came home late she said, 'This has been happening for a few weeks now and I have to ask: do you have a boyfriend? Because if you're meeting him so secretively that you feel you can't bring him home, then he's not any good. He is only out for something that you can't give him. You'll come home pregnant and he'll dump you.' She thought I was having an affair, perhaps with a married man. So to clear my good name I told her I didn't have a boyfriend but was attending classes and had joined the Communist Party. She said she admired me for being stronger than she had been. It was quite significant for her daughter to become a member. From that time forward and throughout my fight as a communist against the Nats and apartheid, my mother supported me.

The communists played a vital role as the only legal party that supported us, the oppressed peoples, against the vicious system of apartheid. People trusted the communists. When they needed help they knew the Party was always ready to assist and wouldn't make them feel inferior, ignorant or humiliated. The communists didn't patronise people but honoured their dignity. They opened crèches for black children in poor areas like Retreat, Elsies River and Langa. They arranged picnics and outings for the black community, particularly at Easter. Though people often went out as a family or with a small group of neighbours, the Party's Progress Club held large picnics. I remember one year the Easter picnic was held at Hout Bay. For people who had no means of transport the Party hired a bus, which would pick them up at various points in the black and coloured communities. That day might have been the only opportunity for some families to get out to the beach with their children.

The Party didn't do these things to buy votes – it wasn't even the time for voting – but because they were the right things to do. The Party was effective because its words and actions for the people never ceased.

People knew the communists were genuine and compassionate. No effort was too much.*

○

When I joined the Party the situation in the world and in South Africa made me ask myself, How could all this happen? How could the Second World War have happened? The Holocaust hit me badly. I first learned about it from a film, watching the Soviets going into Nazi Germany. It wasn't the horror of the bodies already dead, but the emaciated people still alive, just skin and bones. For days I just kept crying. I could not believe that this had been allowed to happen. Why had God not intervened?

And in South Africa: so much heartache and murder and death under apartheid. Our people – the Africans – weren't shoved into ovens as the Nazis had done to the Jews. Instead of the gas chambers, the Nats oppressed our African people in other ways. In fact, we now know that at one stage they might have tried to exterminate blacks had they had the opportunity. African women were afraid to practise birth control because they felt the Nats were trying to sterilise them. At that time many of us talked about a strong connection we saw between Nazi Germany and apartheid South Africa. The blacks were the Jews of South Africa.

So I became sceptical, absolutely sceptical about religion. I didn't see anything to make me believe that above and beyond what happened throughout the world there was some higher being. There was no higher power to stop fascism and Nazism. There was too much taking place that was wrong.

When apartheid really became oppressive, around 1950, I began to question things and stopped attending church. And it wasn't only me. Many of my pals stopped going to church. They couldn't give me a

---

* Formed in 1921, the Communist Party of South Africa (CPSA) initially focused on the concerns of organised and skilled white workers. James La Guma, Alex La Guma's father, played a major role in shifting the Party's focus to blacks. Communists were active in Cape Town politics in the years prior to apartheid, with Cissie Gool and others elected to the City Council in the 1930s and 1940s. By 1945 the Communist newspaper *The Guardian* had a circulation of about 50,000.

reason. The only thing I can think of is that, like me, they knew religion had no impact on the people. In fact, church attendance began to dwindle, especially among the younger generation in Cape Town where religion had always played a big role.

When I attended Communist Party lectures I started to see that religion lacked any positive role in society. People didn't *think*. They just repeated things without debate, argument or discussion. They went to church, read the prayer book, and said the litany, but that's where it ended. At Party meetings we had the freedom to think in discussions and debates. We didn't challenge the Bible, though. My questioning of the faith I had grown up with was something I did on my own. Even my mother, a Sunday-school teacher, couldn't help me make sense of things. Neither she nor my father could persuade me to let go of my questioning and come back to the faith.

When I joined the Communist Party I began to see that the morality I had been taught by my parents was communist morality. You don't just grab in life; you also give. When volunteers were called to do a task in the community, we in the Communist Party had to be among the first to raise our hands. That's one of the points that stuck with me a long time. Give things; give your time; give freely of yourself: that's the most important thing I learned as a communist.

When I joined the Party before it was banned, you could talk openly to people about communism. When the Party was banned in 1950, all that fell away. The Party went underground and you then had to rejoin. The Party had to make sure you knew how to keep quiet. If you were interrogated by the police you were to say, 'I don't belong. I don't know anybody else who belongs.' Loyalty was critical. They couldn't have somebody who was going to spill the beans. I rejoined but that was later, after my marriage to Alex. I never regretted joining – and rejoining – the Communist Party.*

---

* Soon after taking power, the National Party passed the Suppression of Communism Act (1950), which outlawed the Communist Party and allowed for officers or supporters of the Party to be 'named' and their activities and movements restricted. The Party was secretly revived in 1953 as an underground organisation now calling itself the South African Communist Party (SACP).

○

Around this time I left the cigarette factory to become a nurse. I wasn't drawn into nursing by the desire to be a nurse. There was just no other alternative. Teaching and nursing were the only two professions open to coloured women, and I had tried teaching. With time I grew into nursing and it really became a part of me. But when I started, I just wanted to improve my status above that of a factory worker and earn more so I could contribute at home.

My family was so poor that I had to get through the nursing course quickly, pass it without any problems, and go to work. I chose midwifery because general nursing would have taken three years while the midwifery programme was only a year and a half. At the time I thought that I would do general nursing later. As trainee nurses we received board and lodging and £2 a month until we qualified. Out of those £2 I had to buy my uniform and stockings and pay for toiletries and train fare. Then I gave the rest to my parents.

I applied to do the course for nurse-midwives at St Monica's Home, a hospital built in 1917 and run by the Cape Town diocese of the Anglican Church specifically for coloured and black women. When I first applied I couldn't get in because it was difficult to be accepted into the programme. So while I waited to be admitted I took courses in first-aid and home nursing on the advice of the matron of St Monica's. I also borrowed a midwifery book to read up on the terminology. Since I had not studied for some years I really had to put my all into studying because I couldn't afford to fail.

After being admitted, I trained as a midwife for 18 months and lived at St Monica's, which was a small hospital of 32 patients with 12 or 13 nurses in training. At the time mainly coloured nurses trained there, along with a few African nurses. The patients were also coloured, with a few Africans, but whites were in charge. In fact, the only white nurses were the matrons, including Miss Margaret Hoey-Jones, the sister-in-charge, and her assistant, Miss Tilbrook, who looked after the wards. Our consultant gynaecologists and obstetricians were also white. The superintendent and paediatrician of St Monica's was Dr Ethel Barrow, a white female. At that time no coloured or black person could become matron. In fact, my close friend and colleague Dorothy (Dollie) Wiid became the first coloured matron of St Monica's Home only in the 1980s.

The white sisters were from England and when they left the hospital, others from England took their place. All were qualified in general nursing and midwifery, and some had even higher nursing qualifications and experience. One of the sisters told us that on the boat coming over they were instructed in how to treat black people in South Africa – that is, how to keep us down. It was presented to them as a matter of class difference: we were said not to be on their level and so should not be treated in the same way. But when they came here, they found that we shared the same language and other aspects of culture. For the most part these white British sisters treated us well. They were good people, friendly with us, though they were also strict teachers.

You qualified as a nurse-midwife by passing two exams. The training was intense. We trained on patients who came to St Monica's. Their stay was subsidised by the Community Chest, which collected money and then gave assistance to charitable organisations like St Monica's. The same was true at Groote Schuur Hospital. Perhaps some of our patients could have gone to private hospitals, but for most patients that was far too expensive. Those who could pay would make a donation.

$$\bigcirc$$

We coloured trainees shared dormitory rooms attached to the hospital, two to a room. The black trainees were not allowed to live in at St Monica's, even though it was administered by the Anglican Church. Four black trainees stayed in a house just opposite the hospital, where the living conditions were appalling. The matron in charge, Miss Hoey-Jones, was broad-minded and liberal, and she finally fought so that at least one of the black staff nurses could live at St Monica's. The hypocrisy of a religious hospital treating blacks this way was yet one more thing that drove me further and further away from the whole business of religion.

Most of the white sisters treated us well, especially Miss Hoey-Jones who had been there longer. But not all did. Sister Tilbrook, the matron's assistant in charge of the wards, seemed like an SS guard and really treated us badly, so much so that we revolted. She was a hefty woman, with big hips and a wide belt. When we first saw her, we realised she was a bully. She was unfortunately one of those who accepted what they told her on the ship coming over.

Sister Tilbrook constantly hounded us, thus preventing us from getting the time off to which we were entitled. Our only scheduled time-off was one half-day a week, which meant working until eleven o'clock in the morning and then having to be back in the hospital at six that night. We were supposed to wash our patients, wash our babies, do our rough work or cleaning, and after all this be out by eleven. It was just one mad rush all the time.

After a while we got things fine-tuned so that we were able to finish on time. But Sister Tilbrook made things difficult.

'Nurse,' she'd say to me, 'you haven't done that properly. I want you to do the whole ward over again.'

When we finished the extra work she expected us to do, it was so late that we couldn't go home – I had to take three buses all the way from Bo-Kaap to Athlone and then come all the way back. We would only get another half-day off the next week, so that meant working two weeks straight without a break. Before we left we also had to report to Sister Tilbrook, but she'd be at tea and would make us wait. But we taught her a lesson.

One day three of us – Lorenza Fortis, Rose Hector and myself – were criticising Sister Tilbrook while we dished up the patients' food.

'She's come to South Africa and is living the good life, while she's treating us badly,' I said. The other two agreed. I went on to point out that Sister Tilbrook had a habit of standing with her hands on her hips and scolding us.

'While my father was in London during the First World War he went to the East End. He told me that's how the barrow women who sell vegetables in the street behave, walking around with a bag of money hanging over their chest. I wonder if she doesn't come from that lower level?'

'Yes,' the others said. 'She stands with her hands on her hips just like a street woman.'

My God, when we looked up she was right at the door! She'd heard the whole story before walking away.

I said to the girls, 'Look, we're all out. It's over. Not only that, we'll have to go before the Nursing Council and they'll kick us out. You never treat your superiors like this.'

I thought we'd be thrown out of nursing school for sure, so I made an application to become a social worker in the meantime. But before I'd even sent off the forms, Sister Tilbrook changed. She began to help us make the beds, which she had never done before, and carried the bedpans for us. She also helped wash the babies so we could get our work done quickly.

Then she called us into her office. I said to the others, 'Here goes, girls. Our heads are going to roll!'

But Sister Tilbrook started telling us how babies are treated in other countries, for example in Iceland. For babies to become acclimatised they are often left outside for a short period, warmly wrapped, with only their little face showing. I discovered this for myself much later in Moscow with my own grandchildren. Well, I didn't even listen to all the stories she told us. She wasn't lecturing us, but rather trying to be friendly, though she talked down to us as if we were little kids.

I don't think Sister Tilbrook knew *what* to do with us – what to say, how to get round us. After that she treated us better. She didn't ever again talk to us while standing with her hands on her hips. I think she had been shocked and shamed by hearing what we thought of her.

Of course, we congratulated ourselves on our victory. I was always called Hermie because of my surname, but now I was Hermie the Rebel. This was the lesson I had learned from my father: you *never* let people tread on your dignity. You stand up on your hind legs and you oppose them. And if it means being put out, too bad: you move on to something else. That was my attitude then, and that has always been my attitude.

Chapter 6

When I was a teenager I didn't have a keen interest in boys. I'd go out with different guys because I didn't want to get hooked on any one. I was happy to be taken out and maybe have a little flirtation, but nothing serious beyond the next date. I just wanted to have a good time.

Around 1947 or 1948 I went out with a German originally from Hamburg called Walter Zoder. Walter and his brother Willie had escaped from Germany during the Nazi purge of the Jews and came to Cape Town. When war broke out they were rounded up and sent to an internment camp for the duration of the war. He told me about the arguments and fights he and his brother had with others in the camp. He had been a member of the German Communist Party, while some of the other men supported Nazism and fascism.

When the war was over, Walter and I met at a social function of the Progress Club, a Communist Party club mainly for youth, though some older people also came on Saturday nights. You could always go to Progress Club parties to meet old friends and make new ones, find some space and have a discussion. These weekly parties were held to keep youngsters on the straight and narrow path, politically as well as socially. The Party also organised the People's Club, where workers could go during lunch hour and in the evening to meet other workers – not only members of the Party – and read books or political material. When the Nats came to power in 1948, I think the Party realised the election was a warning that it would be banned before long, and so they established these two clubs to build support.

At the Progress Club functions Walter enjoyed dancing with me. The parties were mixed, with blacks and whites mingling freely. I never felt out of place with him. I had never suffered from an inferiority complex because my mother always told me that nobody was better than I was. Many white friends visited our home, so I was comfortable being around Walter and other whites.

Walter became very fond of me. I liked him but was not in love with him – or anybody else for that matter. Sometimes we'd go to his flat in Camps Bay with its beautiful view of the ocean. Walter would make tea, coffee and snacks and we'd listen to music, which he sometimes explained to me. Walter was quite knowledgeable about classical music, and he had a large music library of mostly classical works. His father had played various instruments in one of the German orchestras before the Nazis took power. Sometimes when we were listening to a recording, Walter would say, 'My father played on that record.'

Walter lived with his brother Willie, who was at the time dating Cissie Gool, a beautiful woman and a real fighter as one of our first coloured City Councillors.* She was a longstanding political friend of my future father-in-law, Jimmy La Guma, and a powerful and outspoken advocate for people's rights. When the Nats threatened to repeal the coloured vote in the Cape in the early 1950s, Cissie Gool and others started the Franchise Action Council (Frac). My parents worked as hard in that campaign as they had in the City Council elections for Cissie, going into people's homes and telling them how important the vote was and that everyone must support Cissie Gool. During that period Cissie often came to our house. Once she made a speech at the engagement party of my brother and his fiancée. One of the guests called out, 'Is this a *political* party?' Cissie was a hero in the eyes of the coloured community all over Cape Town. We thought she would be our first black mayor of Cape Town, but because of apartheid she never had the opportunity.

* Zainunnisa 'Cissie' Gool (1897–1963) was first elected to the Cape Town City Council in 1938 and served from 1938 until her death from a stroke in July 1963. She helped lead the Franchise Action Council (FRAC), an alliance of civic organisations opposed to the disenfranchisement of Cape coloured voters.

◯

When Walter and I went out, he was always the gentleman. He often invited my parents to join us for a drive. Once he took us all to Camps Bay to prove to my parents that he had honourable intentions. Walter was a master builder and contractor. He showed us a house he was building, a beautiful mansion with a lovely view of the mountain and the sea. He told my mother that if I married him he would build for me 'the palace of South Africa'. But Walter was about ten years older and I wasn't ready for marriage to any man. When he asked my mother to speak with me, she told him that I must make my own decision. He was very sad when I said that I couldn't commit myself to a stable relationship and rejected his marriage offer.

With the passage of the Immorality Act in 1950, I asked Walter not to visit me any more. 'Look, Walter,' I said, 'what if I'm sitting with you at your house in Camps Bay and we're caught together? You'll go and pay a fine, which you can pay ten times over. But there's only one sentence for me and that's imprisonment.' I wasn't even in love with Walter. How could I go to prison for him?

Walter was keen that we should elope to Germany. I said no. We couldn't live together in South Africa, and I certainly was not going with him to Germany. If I'd been in love I might have considered it, but I wasn't. After that, we still continued to go out occasionally. Though Walter hoped I'd change my mind, I never did. Eventually he returned to Hamburg.

I also briefly dated a man named Manuel. He was the Greek owner of a clean little café near our house in Athlone where people bought the daily papers, magazines, confectionery, cigarettes, and so forth. I met him through my father, who used to have long chats with Manuel when he went to buy the paper. The two of them got on very well. Manuel had a long Greek first name that was difficult to pronounce. When I tried to say it I got lockjaw. So I just called him Manuel.

Manuel also owned two beautiful shops in Paarl and Wellington. He offered to let me manage one of them as my own. But on one occasion I saw that he had a gun under the counter in case anybody tried to break in. I thought, 'He's prepared to kill somebody to save his business.' That didn't go down well with me. But it wasn't the reason I broke off with him.

One night at a party Manuel and I spent a lovely evening dancing and socialising. He guided me in the tango and I quickly learned the steps. But while he was driving me home, he made it clear that he completely disagreed with communists and communist thinking. He said he supported the fascist government of his country and that communists were bad people, even though he knew what my leanings were. So I dropped him like a hot potato and never went out with him again.

I'm not sure what attracted these foreign men to me. I was young and friendly, but I wasn't ready to get involved. They were nice to go out with and have as friends, but I wasn't in love with any of them. I didn't want a boyfriend and I certainly wasn't ready for marriage.

○

Even before I went out with any of these men, my mother talked openly to me about the possibility of falling pregnant. She was afraid the same thing would happen to me as when she had Herbert out of wedlock. She made it abundantly clear that if the guy insisted on sex, I was to tell him to have a bath or take a walk. She said sex was in the mind and did not necessarily have to happen. I'm not sure whether she had made an in-depth study of the matter or just read about it in *Woman's Weekly*.

There was also no birth control at the time. The pill was available only at a later stage when I started midwifery. Condoms weren't widely used or, if they were, I didn't know about them. So from the word go I made it clear to each of the men I dated where the line was drawn. And when they came to our house my mother also gave instructions. 'You look after my daughter,' she said. 'Don't let her come home pregnant.' She was as straight as a line.

It didn't bother me that she said this to them. I knew she was protecting me and dealing with a matter I probably couldn't deal with on my own. She spoke openly about sex with each guy. 'You are taking my daughter out,' she said. 'Just make sure you bring her back in the same condition you found her.' The men never took offence. They were also much older than I was. By the time Alex came around, I think she realised he knew better and I was much older too. If I hadn't learned by then, I never would. My mother always said, 'Remember, *you* are the important one. Nobody's better than you are.'

○

I first met Alex at Trafalgar High School where he was two years ahead of me. He also occasionally visited my brother George at our home on Saturdays. When Alex was in the house I didn't pay him any attention, and he certainly didn't pay any attention to me. I was scrawny and not good-looking. When he came, I grabbed my bicycle and was gone.

It was only later, just before the Communist Party was banned in 1950, that I got to know him at Progress Club social functions. We'd do a little smooching at the party, but nothing serious – just a hug, a kiss and a squeeze. After the party Alex and I went our separate ways and perhaps met again when the Progress Club had another function.

By the time I took up nursing I had lost contact with Alex. While I was finishing my training at St Monica's in 1952, I joked with my friends about my lack of romantic prospects. 'I'm 25, a quarter of a century,' I told them. 'Just put me on the shelf and see that you periodically give me a dust with your duster.'

Then one day as I was walking down Adderley Street, I ran into Alex. We seemed so pleased to see each other. At the end of our chat I said, 'Well, I must dash back. I have to be on duty.'

'When can I see you again?' he said.

'Well, I suppose we'll meet up again as we did today.' I didn't realise the man was fixing a date with me. I was too naïve.

'No,' he said. 'I want something better than that. Can I meet you on Sunday?'

'I'm on duty. I won't be able to come.'

'The next Sunday then.'

'The next Sunday, yes.'

Alex offered to pick me up at St Monica's and take me to his house. But that would mean he'd have to walk from Hanover Street in District Six up the mountain to St Monica's and then both of us walk down again. What was the point? I'm a practical person on the whole. So I said, 'I'll meet you downtown.'

When I came back to St Monica's that afternoon, I said to the girls, 'I've got a date! I'm going out on Sunday.' They were all excited. We were like a lot of old maids, in our mid-twenties and unmarried.

When the time came for the date on Sunday, the girls were all cheering me on. 'Oh Hermie, look at your hair. You look like an old woman! Get your hair right. Make a fashion.'

I got on the bus and met him down the road. We then went to his house to see his mother and father. I'd already met them when my parents worked for his father, Jimmy La Guma, during his election campaign for the City Council more than ten years earlier. I'd also participated in a political meeting his father had held in Athlone. His father knew I was politically active, and I was warmly welcomed when I met the family again. Alex's parents remained in the kitchen while Alex and I sat together having tea.

After half an hour he proposed marriage and I accepted.

It was terrible in one way, because I thought, 'What will he think of me? In the first half-hour he's asked me to marry him and already I've said yes!' I worried that it might make me look loose. But he knew that wasn't the case because of my family and where I came from.

I thought I could make my life with this guy. We had the same interests and a lot in common from our earlier years. We were at school together (he was two years older) and we'd had a bit of a cuddle and squeeze at parties. I also was familiar with his family. I knew how heavily they were involved in politics and I was interested in politics too. I knew both his mother and father already accepted me and that I would fit in with them.

I also had a feeling about Alex that I didn't have with Walter or the others. Alex was my first boyfriend really, the first one I truly cared about. I felt something romantic.

I remember one of my brother George's friends saying, 'How can you marry him? Look at that face!' (Alex was tall and very thin.)

'Oh, I *like* that lean and hungry look!' I said.

At that point in my life it wasn't a matter of kissing, canoodling and holding hands. Back then there wasn't the same emphasis on sex as there is today. I wanted a more mature relationship and to settle down. What is marriage but settling down and living together? You get on with each other and love each other – not by shouting, 'I love you, I love you' – but in a deeper way.

We later used to have gentle arguments about what happened that afternoon.

'What a cheek!' I said. 'You waited just half an hour to propose marriage.'

'That's right,' he'd say. 'But you said yes.'

I said yes because I knew this was the guy for me. And my heavens, I never regretted it!

○

Ours was almost a classic romance. Alex was debonair. He'd sing a song, a sweet song, or recite a poem. I was struck deeply when he recited Cyrano de Bergerac: 'Your name hangs like a bell around my heart. When it rings it says, "Blanche, Blanche, I love you."'

He also strummed on his guitar and sang ballads and love songs just to me. He serenaded me with a popular song called 'Lily of Laguna':

'I know she loves me, I know she likes me, because she said so.

She's my lady love; she's my love, my baby love.

She's my lily of Laguna. She's my lily and my rose.'

Alex was absolutely fun to be around with. We had an active life together. We went to cinema quite a lot as he was especially fond of Westerns. We were also rock 'n' rollers. It was the era when rock 'n' roll and the jitterbug came along. We'd go to a dance in the town hall of Athlone or at a wedding reception where the band was playing the new music, mostly from America. The dancing was vibrant. Alex could easily pull me through his legs, push and turn me, and then throw me over his shoulders. I was quite thin and light at the time, boasting a waste line of 18 inches. I enjoyed being tossed around. Much later in the 1970s when we travelled to Uzbekistan, a jazz band played some music that took us back to our youth and we danced again. Alex swung me around, but said, 'Don't expect me to throw you over my shoulders.' I didn't – by that time I had put on quite a bit of weight.

I appreciated Alex so very much. We worked hard at politics, but we also had great fun. He was warm-hearted towards me and later with our boys as well. His subtle humour was hilarious. I would kill myself laughing at some of the things he'd say in his dry way. I used to tell others, 'I'm living in Bo-Kaap and I've got a boyfriend living in Onder-Kaap' – District Six, lower Cape Town. Bo-Kaap and Onder-Kaap didn't get on very well. The skollie boys, the ruffians of Bo-Kaap, didn't like the men of District Six. But when Alex came visiting, they said, 'Just leave him alone. That's the nurse's boyfriend.'

$$\bigcirc$$

Alex was well known in the community as a young man in the Communist Party who spoke frequently on the Grand Parade before the Party was banned in 1950. He and Lionel Forman joined the Party when they were in their teens.[*] He helped lead the opposition when the Nats introduced apartheid on the buses. Alex used to get up four o'clock each morning to walk to the city, showing others that nobody should travel in the buses. Ultimately the boycott wasn't successful, but he had a lot of support.

Even when he was young, Alex wanted to get involved in politics. He tried to volunteer for the Spanish Civil War in 1938 at the age of 13, but when he went to a recruiting station to register they told him to go away. Though he was tall and lanky, he was clearly only a boy. From an early age he was politically active and an ardent reader. After our marriage we always had *Das Kapital* in the house as well as other volumes of Marx, Engels and Lenin, whom he studied to the core. He knew communism inside-out and was able to debate communism as a philosophy with the best of them.

[*] Lionel Forman (1927–1959), like Alex La Guma, was a communist activist and writer for *New Age* in 1950s Cape Town. As one of the 156 Treason Trialists, Forman co-authored with Solly Sachs *The South African Treason Trial* while he was still on trial.

From the first Alex used his art to express his political ideas. As a young man he did a course in painting at the Hyman Liberman Institute, a cultural organisation in District Six.* Alex was always painting and creating cartoon strips, like the 'Little Libby' series that appeared in *New Age* in the late 1950s. And of course he wrote stories, though his mother didn't seem to appreciate them at the time. When Alex first started writing, she didn't realise that her son was a future writer in the making and threw his stories away.

○

I was doing a three months' stint of night duty as a qualified midwife when Alex and I were courting. One morning after I finished night duty, the day nurses who were just coming on told me, 'Staff nurse, the police have been ringing here. They want you to come down to Caledon Square for an interview.' Caledon Square is the main police station in Buitenkant Street.

'Oh, blow the police,' I said. 'I've not committed any crime. Tell them I'm leaving night duty and going to sleep.' I really didn't care.

One Friday morning just after eight when I had given the night report to Matron Hoey-Jones, she told me that two plainclothes policemen from the Special Branch wanted to speak with me. 'I put them in my office,' she said. 'They're waiting for you there.'

I didn't have a clue what it was all about, but I wasn't nervous. My only thought was that I hadn't committed a crime. I was met in her office by a large coloured man and a thin, slightly shorter white man. When we were seated the white man said, 'You are Blanche Herman.'

'Yes, I am.'

'Alex La Guma is your boyfriend.'

'Yes he is.' Only then it hit me: this was political. So immediately I got my defences up.

---

* The Hyman Liberman Institute was considered a centre of 'high culture' in District Six in the 1930s and 1940s. Begun in 1934 as a reading room and community centre for the poor through a bequest by Cape Town mayor and businessman Hyman Liberman, the Institute offered opportunities for education and discussion.

'Well, we have come to tell you to break off your association with Alex. He's a communist. He is bad for you.' (They didn't know that I was a communist too.)

'I will not break off any association with Alex,' I said. 'He is my boyfriend. I am engaged to him, and I am marrying him.'

'We can make your life very difficult if you continue to associate with him,' the Special Branch man said.

'You can make my life as difficult as you like. There will be no breaking off my relationship with Alex.'

'Well!' the man said. 'So be it on your head.'

I later learned that the white man was called 'Spyker', meaning 'nail' in Afrikaans. In fact, Spyker van Wyk and his brother Andries, who was assigned to watch us later, were both Special Branch men. Spyker was tall, thin, and gaunt, with a long face. He was probably younger than his brother, but more violent. He went on to become one of the most infamous torturers of the apartheid regime.* The other man, a big, hefty coloured fellow, was called Tiny. Among the coloured community, particularly in the Cape, there is a custom of giving people nicknames. If you are coloured but have fair skin, they call you Whitey; and if you are big and hefty, they call you Tiny.

I wasn't intimidated by these men. I was angry. 'How could they?' I thought. I told Matron Hoey-Jones what they had come to see me about.

Though she didn't say anything in reply, she didn't need to. We were a close-knit family at the hospital. I knew she supported me. That is why several years later when we held a street march against apartheid in nursing I didn't have to say, 'Matron, I hope you will support me in the march.' I just phoned her and said, 'I'm going to have a march,' and she turned up.

When I told Alex about the visit from these two men, he laughed.

'They don't know about *you*, do they?' he said. 'They're following me.' Yet he was also astounded because he didn't think the Nats would go so far.

---

* Hernus J.P. 'Spyker' van Wyk had a long and infamous career as an interrogator and torturer in the Special Branch.

This happened in 1953, a year before we were married and three years after the Party had been outlawed by the Suppression of Communism Act. The Nats had long known who the communists were because they had been watching us. They kept their eyes on Alex in meetings and speeches on the Grand Parade. It turned out that those two policemen meant what they said, because the Special Branch really led me a dance after my marriage. They made my life as difficult as they had promised.

◯

Alex and I were engaged for about two years after he proposed to me. In those days, at the ages of 29 and 27 we may have been considered old for getting married, but we waited until we were both mature enough to settle into life together in the struggle and have a family. We also couldn't get married soon after our engagement as people do today: we had to work and save.

We were married on Saturday, 13 November 1954. I didn't want to have a big wedding because I felt we couldn't afford it. Though my parents were struggling, my mother insisted. I was the Herman's daughter and a member of the community, so that was it. We had a big wedding, with about fifty people at the church and two hundred at the reception.

We were married at St Mark's Anglican Church in Athlone, the church I attended while growing up. Neither of us was religious. I am an agnostic and Alex was an outspoken atheist, as was his father, Jimmy. We got married in a church for the sake of my parents and the community. Jimmy La Guma, the La Guma family, and even my mother played a big role locally. There are certain things you do in the community to get their support. And among these is that you get married in a church, even if you're not religious. Alex's father said to him, 'You've got a duty to the community. You work in the community, and you want that community to follow what you're saying. You must be part of them, or else the people will say, "Yes, you want us to follow you and what you're saying. But you don't do what we believe in. How can we support you?" So it's necessary that you do what the community would do.'

I bought my wedding dress at a shop called Rejane in Adderley Street, Cape Town. It cost about 45 pounds. They let me pay in instalments, and by the time I got married I had paid it off in full. When I first saw the dresses in the window, I knew exactly what I wanted. It was beautiful. The material was heavily ruched from the bottom up where the cotton is pulled into creases on the whole skirt, right around. I had to have a veil and a train, though not too long. When I went to fit my wedding gown, the lady making the dress said, 'Here she comes with her wasp figure.' I was very thin – an 18 inch waist – healthy and happy, but thin.

At some weddings the groom – or the man who was supposed to be the groom – wouldn't pitch up at all. He'd leave the girl waiting. So I said to Alex: 'Look here. When you drive past our house on the way to the church, make sure all the cars are hooting to let me know you're coming. That way I'll know I can leave the house and that you'll be waiting for me when I walk down the aisle. Because if I'm at the church before you and you don't turn up, I'll kill you.'

It was a lovely, short service – no ring-bearer or flower girl, no special message from the priest. The nurses from St Monica's all came to the church and formed a guard of honour for me. As they stood in parallel lines facing each other with their arms up and fingers touching, Alex and I walked through.

Chapter 7

'Here comes Batman!'

After our wedding Alex and I stayed with my parents at their house in Gleemoor, Athlone. We helped pay the rates, electricity and water, so that we could save towards buying our own house. But we could never save much: Alex went and got himself involved in politics!

Right after we married I wanted to show off my cooking skills to him. I thought I'd make bean stew for our first meal. Alex was fond of beans – not green beans, but dry bean stew. Both of us came from a working-class background where the main dish for the week was usually a stew. I wanted to make a stew for Alex just the way I saw my mother make it. But the problem was that my mother hadn't let me learn to cook because she'd been so protective of me all along. She was afraid I would burn myself on our cast-iron stove, which had several bad cracks in it. My first stew was quite a joke. First of all, I had no sense of proportion. I cooked a whole pound of beans in a pot, with no room for the gravy. The beans swelled and the gravy almost spilled over. My mother tried to tell me I was using far too many beans, but of course I asked her not to interfere. I was the wife cooking my husband's first meal and I wanted to show my skills.

When Alex and I ate the stew we nearly choked. It was absolutely dry. I just nudged him with my elbow and said, 'I'll make a better dish next time.'

He was good about it. 'Never mind,' he said. 'Cooking is my hobby. I'll do the cooking.'

He *was* a good cook, who had learned from his mother. Whenever he put something into the pot it came out well. Little did we know that eventually cooking would become his permanent responsibility when he was under house arrest because I was seldom home, running around delivering babies and keeping the wolf from the door by earning a living.

○

When I finished midwifery training, I did domiciliary work in the district, delivering babies at home. I went around on a bicycle to my patients. Before I got the bicycle I had to walk long distances with my delivery bag or take the bus. With the bicycle I could fit everything on to the carrier and travel far if I needed to. I even did deliveries at two or three in the morning. Riding home on my bike through the neighbourhoods was quite safe. Later on, when Alex was heavily involved in political work and often detained, some of my friends contributed anonymously to purchasing a motor that fitted on to the back of the bicycle. I could still pedal, but most of the time I just switched on the motor and off I went. The only problem was that the motor was exposed, and when it rained I couldn't use it.

Nurse La Guma on duty

I must have looked quite funny on the bike. When it was cold I wore my nurse's veil and navy blue cape with red trim. With the cape and veil flying about in the wind, I looked like Batman! When people saw me, they used to say, 'Here comes Batman!' Everybody knew it was Nurse La Guma coming along.

○

After a birth I would visit the mother and baby twice a day for the first three days, taking temperatures and checking for infection. If there was cause for concern, I made a third visit around five in the afternoon. If the baby's temperature went up, I called the doctor.

Simply keeping a baby alive was a huge challenge in the poorer communities. Infant mortality rates for black and coloured infants were extremely high.[*] Most of these children died of malnutrition. The mothers were malnourished, so the milk was malnourished. Even when mothers were given artificial powders and milk at the clinic, they couldn't prepare the food. The water tap may have been a long way off or there were no facilities for boiling water. I knew sometimes when I delivered a baby that I was bringing it into a world of hunger and starvation. It was a slow death. But what could I do? I couldn't shove it back. After all, a baby has a right to be born.

Most of the patients paid a small fee of £3 for antenatal care, the delivery, and ten days of visits after the birth. I also had a few wealthy white patients whom I charged £8 or £10 to help pay for the mothers who couldn't afford the care. These white women called me because I could provide the same care as white nurses (or even better), who charged £25. They'd find me through doctor's referrals or might ask their maid who had delivered her babies and she'd say, 'Get Nurse La Guma. I had her, she's very good.'

Some of the white women treated me with respect, though not all. I was sent to one white woman by her doctor because I think the doctors were trying to give me work. The woman lived in Pinelands where only the wealthy lived. I delivered her, and while I was bathing the baby one

---

[*]   Infant mortality rates from 1950 to 1953 were 91 of 1 000 for coloureds, and 227 of 1 000 for black Africans.

morning her daughter, who must have been four or five years old, came up to me. 'Nurse, do you like Dr Verwoerd?' I'm sure she had been sent to ask me this question. Verwoerd, the architect of separate development, was in power then.

I said, 'No darling, I don't. Dr Verwoerd is not good to me. He treats me very badly, and I don't see how I can like him.'

The mother never booked me again. She took on another coloured nurse who didn't oppose apartheid the way I did. Some of our nurses had a docile and solicitous attitude. But I didn't. I felt that when I lost such a patient, I wasn't losing anything. I hadn't lost my dignity.

$$\circ$$

For the birth of my own first child in February 1956, I went to stay with Alex's mother, Wilhemina, at her house. She wanted me to be there since it would be her first grandchild, while my mother already had grandchildren. So in the week or two before Eugene was born, I shared a double bed with my mother-in-law while Alex and his father shared another room.

I went into labour at about three in the morning. My mother-in-law got all excited and my father-in-law went with me and Alex in a taxi to St Monica's. Eugene arrived at eight in the morning, weighing nine pounds, and was delivered by my good friend Dolly.

Unfortunately, Eugene's baptism did not go as smoothly. My mother and mother-in-law both felt Eugene had to have a baptism, though neither Alex nor I was religious. I asked my father-in-law what to do.

'What does it matter?' he said. 'Does it do any harm having him baptised? It will make Mommy [La Guma] happy. It will make your Mommy happy. We can have a party. After he's baptised, then raise him your way.'

Just as with our wedding, we had Eugene (and later Barto) baptised in the Anglican Church out of a sense of duty to our community. On a day off work I went to St Mark's Church in Athlone to arrange for Eugene's baptism. The main priest wasn't there and another priest was filling in. I said to him that I'd like to have Eugene baptised.

The priest was rude to me. He looked at me with a sneer and said, 'Don't you work?'

'Yes, I do work. I work hard.'

'But what are you doing here today?'

He told me I should come back on Sunday morning after church to register Eugene. Then I lost my temper. I wasn't over-enthusiastic about the baptism in the first place.

'I am working at St Monica's Home. I happen to have a day off,' I said. 'St Monica's Home is run by the diocese of the Anglican Church. I am a confirmed and baptised member of the church. But if you don't want to baptise Eugene, I don't need the baptism certificate. The law says only that he must have a birth certificate. So I don't need you.' I stormed out.

As I was walking away he shouted, 'Mother! Mother! Please come back!' He practically begged me to register Eugene, and I did so.

$$\circ$$

In August 1956, black women initiated a nationwide women's anti-pass campaign. I was going to Pretoria to join in the main march but then Eugene, six months old, decided to get bronchitis. Though Cape Town had its own march to Parliament, I couldn't even join that. Eugene was just too ill.

During that time women met to strategise on how best to oppose the pass laws. We coloureds weren't especially involved in the anti-pass campaign because we didn't have to carry a pass. Black men carried passes and now the regime was trying to introduce the pass to black women.* We opposed this from the word go. We coloureds participated because we knew that in the final analysis the pass would come to coloureds and Indians as well.

While the main anti-pass march was held in Pretoria on 9 August,

---

* With African women moving to the cities in the 1940s and 1950s, the Nationalist government in 1952 passed the paradoxically named Abolition of Passes and Coordination of Documents Act which, in fact, required African women to carry the same kind of reference books as black males. The Federation of South African Women (Fedsaw) fought the passes with demonstrations, most famously the August 1956 march on government offices in Pretoria.

there were other marches locally. Everybody went because there was such strong opposition to the pass, a document that didn't even give black people the right to exist.

Whenever we marched, the children marched along with us. We put them in prams or carried babies and younger children on our shoulders. Often babies went from one person to another. Everybody was an aunt or uncle. People would help by walking with your children a way, then giving them back to you. Eventually you'd ask, 'Who's got him now?' 'Oh, So-and-so.' At the end of the march you'd fetch your child. We felt absolutely secure. Those who marched were all on our side. Eugene and Barto went on many marches. We tried to teach them from an early age what their future role must be. They were not to think only of themselves but of the other children.

After the 1956 march, the women said how nervous they'd been. They didn't know whether they'd be arrested or even shot because that was the first time women had marched in open defiance. While there had been a Defiance Campaign in 1952, this was the first time women put themselves on the line. Across the board, the whole struggle was relentless. It was a continual struggle, night and day, every day, everywhere we were. It had to be.

Chapter 8

'The feeling was, They can never kill 156 people'

One morning at about nine, two Special Branch men dressed in civilian clothes came to see Alex at my parents' house where we were living. When I told them that Alex was working at *New Age*, they asked me to call him home.

Our house was on the corner of Louisvale and Boeschoten roads. The SB men had come through the main gate in Louisvale Road and weren't aware there was another gate on Boeschoten Road that led from the backyard into the room where Alex and I lived at the rear of the house. While Alex travelled all the way home from town by bus, the men just sat in the front room like a couple of bumps on a log. I stayed in the kitchen with my mother and her friend, Mrs Jutzen, who had popped in for a quick visit. We weren't going to serve these men tea or make them comfortable.

When I looked through the kitchen window I saw Alex coming down Boeschoten Road – not Louisvale Road, which he would normally take – and knew that he was aware of what was happening. I also knew I had to protect a special document in a bedroom cupboard – we called it the black book. I'm fairly certain this document related to the idea of the Black Republic, the communist plan for revolution in South Africa, developed during meetings that his father Jimmy attended in the Soviet Union in the 1920s. Alex told me this was a special book that no one should lay hands on – not only the Special Branch, but anybody else for that matter.

I kept my cool and walked calmly down the passage to our bedroom.

I found the document in its black cover and placed it in a paper carrier. Fortunately our room had a back door that opened onto the yard, as did the kitchen. I exited via the back door and re-entered through the kitchen without the policemen ever seeing me. Once in the kitchen, I calmly placed the paper carrier into the open bag that Mrs Jutzen had left on the floor, not saying anything, and waved my hand, indicating she should leave.

When Alex entered from the front entrance he said in his usual polite way, 'Good morning, gentlemen. What may I do for you?'

I can't recall what else was said but the policemen searched our bedroom, including all the cupboards and drawers. They didn't search any other part of the house, since my mother stood up to them by making it clear that only one room belonged to Alex. They found nothing that could incriminate him.

This was the first time we were raided by the police. They weren't as thorough as they would become in the 1960s. They didn't arrest or even question Alex. They had called him there only to be present in case they found something.

Alex's first detention came in June 1955 when a group of about sixty Western Cape delegates travelling to the famous Congress of the People in Kliptown was stopped at a police roadblock at Beaufort West in the Karoo. The group had left Cape Town secretly at night. Though the police managed to take all their names, there were more delegates than the police could handle, so some escaped and made it to Kliptown.

Among those who decided not to escape were Alex and Amy Thornton. Like Alex, Amy was an experienced political activist. The two were more seasoned in dealing with the police, and remained with the less-experienced delegates. Those who stayed were confined to their vans, which the police had escorted into the yard. They were able to make phone calls to friends, to ask them to bring food. Later, they heard somebody outside the fence singing 'The Internationale', which only a communist would sing. Suspecting it was somebody for them, Alex and Amy came out of the van and discovered they weren't even being guarded. There were too many detainees for the few police to keep an eye on all of them, so Alex and Amy escaped through an opening in the fence. Outside they discovered that the person singing was their comrade Jack Tarshish, who had brought money from the Party for the delegates to buy food.

After Jack left, Alex and Amy had to sneak back *into* detention. They decided just to go through the front entrance of the police station. When the police saw them walk in, they were shocked. How on earth could the two prisoners be standing right in front of them when they were supposed to be at the back in the van? These police were not members of the Special Branch, though. These were just ordinary officers serving in a little town in the Karoo.

○

On 4 December 1956, I was called out at night to attend to an emergency case. After the birth I stayed the night to make sure the mother was completely stabilised and came home at nine the next morning. My mother was holding Eugene, then ten months old. Through her tears she told me that Alex had been arrested at four that morning and charged with treason. She said there had been a simultaneous arrest of dozens of activists throughout the country. Each one had a knock on the door at four and each was charged with treason.

I was exhausted, having been awake all night. I wasn't ready to face the reality of Alex's arrest. When I phoned the *New Age* office to tell them that Alex had been arrested, Brian Bunting answered and said that everybody at the office had also been detained, including his wife Sonia.[*]

After I had packed toiletries and clothing for Alex, Brian rang to say that those arrested had already left by plane from the Youngsfield Military Airport in Wynberg. Now they were gone altogether. Where was Alex? I called back to *New Age* to speak with our advocate, Lionel Forman, who also worked for the paper, but was told that Lionel had also been arrested. Everybody had been taken.

Eventually we learned that those arrested had been flown by military

---

[*]   *New Age* was the longest-running left-wing newspaper in the country during the apartheid era, appearing weekly from 1937 to 1962 and changing its name every time it was banned.

plane to Johannesburg. That same morning the newspapers carried headlines about the dawn raids and arrests. All 156 arrestees were members of the Congress Movement and many were also members of the Communist Party. They were charged with treason for fighting apartheid, especially for producing the Freedom Charter of people's basic rights at the Congress of the People at Kliptown. According to the regime, the Freedom Charter was treasonable. Yet Alex had been prevented by the police themselves from even going to Kliptown.

When Alex and other Cape Town trialists returned just before Christmas during a break in the trial, Communist Party members Jack and Naomi Barnett hosted a big party for them at their house in Higgovale, a smart suburb on the lower slopes of Table Mountain with fabulous views of the bay. Jack was a leading architect who later won many awards for his building designs throughout South Africa, including the Baxter Theatre in Rondebosch. It was a wonderful party. All the Treason Trialists from Cape Town and their spouses were there, including Jack and Rica Hodgson, Sonia and Brian Bunting, Fred and Sarah Carneson, Lionel and Sadie Forman, Ben and Mary Turok, and Reg and Hettie September, whom we later lived with in London.

There was a special joy in being part of this group of people; we were all in the same boat. With so many people on trial we were concerned about the future. The reality of it hit me when I read the headline 'Treason can carry death sentence'. We didn't know what would happen. But the feeling was, 'They can never kill 156 people.' There would be an outcry. And by this time the world was already crying out. So we set all of this aside for one night and had fun. And did I have a marvellous time! I had bought a beautiful red dress, and while I was dancing the rumba with Alex the band played 'The Lady in Red' specially for me.

Our own house was also the scene of some wonderful Christmas parties, alive with the laughter and noise of hundreds of comrades from all over. In fact, one time when I went outside I couldn't get back into the house. At twelve o'clock we sang 'The Internationale' and all the ANC freedom songs. By two or three in the morning everybody was thoroughly exhausted and made their way home. But during the Treason

Trial people from out of town stayed over at our home. As communists we never turned anyone down. People would sleep on blankets, chairs, a mattress on the floor, whatever, and not just for one night. They'd stay for two or three weeks. One year we had seven house guests in our little place.

○

Early in January the Treason Trial recommenced. Some Cape Town wives went to Jo'burg to be near their husbands. I was among those who stayed in Cape Town and waited for recesses when Alex returned home. I was building up a practice and didn't want to relocate to Jo'burg. I also felt I must give Eugene a stable home.

Eugene was ten months when Alex was arrested and more than three years old when Alex was finally released from the trial in 1959. I wrote to Alex every day, putting a little scribble in from Eugene as his contribution, telling his Daddy that he loved and missed him. I felt it was important to let Alex know that we had not forgotten him. During the recesses, when Alex was not at the *New Age* office, he spent all of his spare time bonding with Eugene – holding him, bathing him, changing his clothes, and telling him that he was his Daddy. When Alex returned to the trial, I would remind Eugene all about his Daddy by showing him photos of Alex.

Though life was tough for us during the Treason Trial, I always remembered there were many of us enduring a similar difficulty. It was good to belong to this loyal family who fought the regime, which was in fact afraid of us. Though we were few in the Cape, we were a close-knit and warm community. We truly loved each other.

Chapter 9

'Don't be satisfied with the crumbs. Demand the whole cake'

While Alex was away at the Treason Trial, I had my own fight on my hands with the attempt of the Nationalist government to impose apartheid on the nursing profession. White nurses had always been considered superior to black nurses, regardless of experience or qualifications. An experienced black nurse received less pay than a white trainee nurse, and could not sit on the Nursing Association or Nursing Council. At St Monica's Home no coloured or black person was allowed to become the matron.

Prior to 1957, these conditions existed in practice, though not in law. Neither black doctors nor black nurses could attend to a white patient in a hospital. In fact, Groote Schuur, the biggest hospital in Cape Town, did not take black nurses to train. Along with other coloured and black nurses and midwives, I had to train at Somerset Hospital in Green Point. At a meeting at St Monica's Home in 1950, a white consultant gynaecologist told us that the government wanted us to have everything for ourselves, including our own hospitals. He was, in other words, trying to indoctrinate us about 'separate development', which would crudely bring apartheid to its full conclusion.

In 1957, legislation was proposed to put nursing apartheid into the statute books.* The white South African Nursing Association planned

---

* The 1957 the Nursing Amendment Act was proposed to bring nursing in line with the larger policy of apartheid. White nurses, especially Afrikaners, were determined to raise their status through improvements in pay, conditions and qualifications not available to black nurses and by establishing stronger credentials as a profession. They felt their control of the nursing profession was being threatened by the rapid increase in black nurses following the Second World War.

to have black nurses write different exams. These and other changes would have suggested we were less qualified and thus prevented us from becoming members of the International Council of Nurses.

When the 1957 Nursing Amendment Bill was discussed in Parliament, we organised nationally to oppose it. The inaugural meeting took place in Johannesburg with the goal of coordinating our work in the provinces. We broke away from the white South African Nursing Association and from the Nursing Council and formed the Federation of South African Nurses and Midwives. We published *Nursing News* to inform nurses what the bill meant if it became law. And we followed the slogan of the Communist Party and the ANC: 'It is better to die fighting on your feet, than to live for ever on your knees.'

In Cape Town we formed the Cape Town Nurses and Midwives Vigilance Committee. I called meetings and mobilised nurses, sneaking into hospitals to tell nurses how badly they'd be treated if the bill became law and legalised discrimination in the profession. In most hospitals the white matrons were fully in favour of these draconian laws and wouldn't allow me inside because nurses were not supposed to take part in politics. So I had to use lookouts to inform me when the white matron or sister-in-charge of the ward was coming. If caught, I could be imprisoned for sedition.

Nancy Dick, a white social worker, drove me to the hospitals and looked after little Eugene in the car while I was busy inside campaigning and dodging the white matron. Once inside the hospital ward I acted as if I was a visitor coming to see a patient. I'd talk with the nurses while they were with patients, saying, 'Come on, get going! Pull up your socks and get to the street demonstration.' We also hired a hall in Mowbray for evening meetings where I spoke to full houses of a hundred or more nurses. Many were receptive, though some were docile and afraid. At a TB hospital in Westlake, I got caught in the wrong place. The matron came through the door at one end of the ward while I was at the other. Fortunately, a large window with sash cords stood open on one side and I jumped out. I just went flying through the open window. Luckily, it was not so high that I injured myself. Nancy was waiting for me with the car running and off we drove. St Monica's Home was the only Cape Town hospital that fully supported us, even though the sisters-in-charge were white. The matron, Miss Hoey-Jones, joined us when we held a protest march through the city streets, as did one of the sisters and the secretary. These three were also members of the Black Sash. The march was the first of its kind in the history of our profession in Cape Town. We were quite impressive, walking in a dignified manner in our nurses' uniforms and red-lined navy blue capes.

I also wrote articles for progressive publications like *New Age*. I was really hell-bent on putting a stop to these changes. I poured my emotions into those articles, and Alex smoothed them off in revision. In a June 1957 article titled 'Nursing Apartheid Will Ruin a Noble Profession', I likened the proposed bill to the 1953 Bantu Education Act. I pointed out that it would place all 'Non-European' nurses on a separate nursing register, restrict election for nursing councils and boards to 'European citizens', and stipulate a different standard of training for non-white nurses. The bill even mandated different uniforms and insignia. Apartheid in the nursing profession would also prevent us from being able to nurse abroad because of different standards for black and coloured nurses. I exposed the 'unadulterated racism' of white nursing leaders who said such things as the 'non-European nurse was a good technician at most' but not a 'real nurse' or 'You cannot have one standard for a highly developed race and the same standard for a lower developed race'.

When the Afrikaans Nurses' League claimed that 'centuries of tradition and culture and civilisation' determined the European nurses' 'superior status', I made clear in no uncertain terms the inequality in facilities, training and opportunities between Europeans and non-Europeans.

A few years later I was banned for having one of my articles in my possession because it appeared in a banned publication, though neither the article nor the publication was originally banned. Albie Sachs, who was then a young lawyer in Himie Bernadt's legal team, took my case to the Appeal Court in Bloemfontein and kept me out of prison by successfully arguing for a suspended sentence.[*]

At one point I was called in by the Cape Town division of the South African Nursing Council. They knew I was arranging meetings and rallying the nurses because there were whistle-blowers telling them so. The Nursing Council wanted to stop me from calling a general nurses' strike, which in fact I had threatened to do and even take beyond Cape Town.

Though the Nursing Council publicly stated that they opposed nursing apartheid, they actually didn't want to do anything. They were afraid that if they took that risk they'd lose their jobs or, worse, would be banned. They were weak and two-faced. And that is precisely what I said when I met with them.

'It's very sad and cruel to say, "We're for the people,"' I said. 'That doesn't mean a thing. What are you doing to stop apartheid?'

In the end we were not successful. The 1957 Nursing Amendment Act became law, segregating black (African, coloured, Indian) and white nurses according to race on the Nursing Council register, establishing 'advisory boards' for coloured (including Indian) and black nurses attached to the white Nursing Council, and even prescribing separate uniforms, badges, and other insignia. Yet we managed to claim two small but significant victories: 'differential training' was removed from the bill so that black and white nurses continued to be qualified by the same examinations, and in response to our vigorous protests, the state dropped the requirement that all nurses carry identity numbers, part of a larger scheme to have black women carry passes. We had stood up and fought nursing apartheid every step of the way. 'Don't be satisfied with crumbs,' we always said. 'Demand the whole cake.'

---

[*]　Albie Sachs (born 1935) began practice as an advocate at the Cape Bar at the age of 21. The bulk of his work involved defending persons charged under security laws, many of whom faced the death sentence. He was subjected to banning orders and twice placed in solitary confinement for extended periods. In 1966 he went into exile. In 1994 he was appointed by President Mandela to the newly established Constitutional Court.

'*The non-White nurses, and all other democrats in the nursing world, have been placed beside the millions of other South Africans struggling against Nationalist "baasskap" and apartheid for the right to live as free and dignified citizens of this country. With enough determination, the bright flame of Florence Nightingale's lamp will rise to dispel the darkness that has so overwhelmed a noble profession.*'

– Blanche La Guma, *Nursing News*, July 1957

Chapter 10

'The assassin apparently wanted to kill two birds with one stone'

One Friday night in 1958 during a recess in the Treason Trial, Alex was at home typing in his study. We'd recently purchased a house in a newly established housing estate in Athlone called Garlandale. We were able to do this with the generous help of our friends Jack Tarshish and Athol Thorn, both of whom insisted on giving us money rather than lending it to us, and Ben and Mary Turok, who helped furnish the house. Alex's room faced the street in front of the house. His father was relaxing with a book on a bed in an adjacent room. Jimmy often came to visit, sometimes staying after a political meeting and only going home later. I was busy changing Eugene, who was two years old, in the other bedroom.

As I couldn't afford to buy good curtains, we had only a thin lace curtain on the window. The light was on in Alex's room. Someone standing in the road could see him clearly.

It was about nine o'clock when the first shot was fired.

When I heard the shot, I left Eugene in the cot and rushed into Alex's room.

'Good God,' I said. 'What's happening?'

Alex passed it off, by saying, 'Ah, don't bother. It must be some kids playing with a pellet gun in the street.'

'Surely not at this hour of the night,' I said. 'It's nine o'clock.'

Alex stood up and with the light still on we looked on the floor for the pellet. But as he got up, the second shot came through the window and caught him, just nipping his neck.

'Damn it!' he said, grabbing the back of his neck. Blood flowed through his hand on to his collar. Realising what was happening, he quickly switched off the light.

By a hair's breadth they'd missed killing him, just grazing his skin near the occipital bone at the base of his skull. Jimmy came out to see what was going on. One of the shots had come through the door into his room. The assassin or assassins apparently wanted to kill two birds with one stone.

Alex and Jimmy walked to the Athlone police station to report the matter. They travelled in the dark over the same bridge from where the shots had been fired. There were no streetlights because Garlandale was a new area. Though I was afraid they'd be shot at again, nothing happened. Nothing happened at the police station, either, because when they reported the incident, the police didn't even take notice.

On Monday when Alex went into work at *New Age*, he received a note printed on glossy white paper that read, 'Sorry we missed you. We'll call again.' Signed, 'The Patriots.' He took the letter to the police station, and it was only then that the police came to our house to investigate. They found a bullet lodged in the wall above where my father-in-law had been relaxing on the bed. A little lower and the bullet would have hit Jimmy. Another bullet was found on the floor where Alex had been sitting, having landed there after ricocheting off the metal frame of the window.

We knew the attempt on Alex's life was the work of the Special Branch. Alex was a danger to the apartheid regime as a high-profile activist and writer, though of course they were after others as well. Because he was so visible from the street that night, it must have been convenient for them to make the attempt on his life. They had no doubt used a high-powered gun because from where they stood and fired it was quite a distance to our house. No culprits were ever found and no official explanation was ever tendered. Our lawyers could do nothing.

○

At this time I wanted another baby. I thought to myself, 'I'm able to carry out my profession with one child and have enough love left for another baby.' I also felt a sibling would be good for Eugene, who was being spoiled by my mother. He was only ten months old when his father was arrested, and I feared he would grow up feeling sorry for himself. On 2 April 1959 our second child, Barto, was born.

While Alex was away at the Treason Trial and I was busy with my nursing, I depended upon my parents to care for the children. When I was out late on a case, the children stayed with them. I'd come home at two or three in the morning and the house would be dark, with not a sound of a child breathing. It really got to me. I was so lonely then, without children to go home to and kiss on their little foreheads. So I went to my parents and took my children back. My father said, 'We've raised all of you, and now you think that we're not capable of raising your children.' But he didn't understand my feeling. I wanted my children with me.

I then asked various women to come and look after Eugene and Barto. They came from farms to the city, needing work, and stayed with us because when Alex was away I needed somebody to be there at night when I was called out. I had some real characters helping me – old and young, town and country, drunk and sober. Some of them treated the children badly and were rough with the boys – yelling and swearing and even hitting them. One older woman, a granny, really drank. One day when I was working I took Eugene, who was about four, to a rough area of Athlone. Before I went into one house he said, 'I know this place, Mommy. Mrs B–– comes here to drink cool drinks.' He was pointing at a shebeen!* When I asked her to leave I took her to her daughter, with whom she lived. At the time I was having to buy a lot of food without really knowing why. When I told her daughter I was letting her mother go, she said, 'But Nurse, you have now deprived us of the food my mother used to take from your house.' Eventually I asked my mother and father to help out again. Eugene and Barto were thrilled to be looked after by their grandparents. And why not? They spoiled the boys.

---

*   An informal, unlicensed tavern.

Chapter 11

'What prisoner can receive strawberries and cream?'

One night shortly after the Sharpeville Massacre in March 1960, we woke up in a fright at about two in the morning. Men were hammering on the doors and windows, shouting, 'Open up!' Alex and I knew it was the Special Branch. I went to the front door while Alex went to the back. When I opened the door, two men in civilian clothes rushed in. The three of us went to the kitchen where we found Alex with men pointing their guns at him, shouting, 'Where are the papers?' Eugene, who was three, came running in and said, 'Don't shoot my Daddy! My Daddy's a good Daddy!' It was horrible.

The police arrested Alex, but not before turning the whole house upside down in their search for documents. Apartheid laws were appearing thick and fast and we'd produce our leaflets accordingly. The security police were always on the lookout for anything that might be useful to them. I could only stand there watching and holding the children, who by this time had wakened.

While there were mass arrests under the state of emergency declared on 30 March, Alex, Reg September and others were actually arrested and detained *before* then.* Alex's father Jimmy was arrested a few days later. After the arrests Hettie September and I didn't know where to find our husbands. We phoned Caledon Square, the main police station, and were sent from pillar to post. It was a gruelling day. I had to leave

---

* During the 1960 State of Emergency, which lasted until 31 August, more than 1,600 people were detained under a new law that provided for detention without trial. Those detained without charge prior to the State of Emergency, such as Alex La Guma and Reg September, were actually held illegally – essentially kidnapped by the police.

the boys with my mother and mother-in-law while I went searching. Our lawyers couldn't find our husbands, either. We heard rumours that people had seen them being shipped off to Robben Island, but our men weren't there. Eventually our lawyers discovered that Alex, Reg and others – whites, coloureds and Africans – were being held at the notorious Roeland Street jail in Cape Town. We immediately went to visit them.

When we entered we were greeted by a tall, fence-like structure separating us from the men. When I saw them I said tearfully, 'Good Lord. What's wrong?' The men were in a shocking state. Alex looked like a lunatic who had just escaped from the asylum. His hair was long and his beard had grown. He had a wild look. He'd always kept himself clean, but now he and the other men stank. They had been grabbed by the police without the chance to take any clean clothes with them. Several of the women were in tears. Even I got a lump in my throat.

'What happened?' Alex said to me. 'Why did you people just leave us here?'

They thought we didn't care a damn and had just dumped them. In the early days of detention one could easily form that impression. I felt the same way when I was later detained.

The visit was difficult because it wasn't only political prisoners who came out to see their visitors, but also common criminals. Our conversations were drowned out by the noise of everybody shouting. Half the time we didn't know what was being said. But at least we saw our men.

After the visit Hettie September, Sadie Forman, and I went to see Margaret Ballinger, one of the 'Native Representatives' in Parliament for the Liberal Party, and presented our complaints. We wanted to see them properly treated and in better condition next time. She raised the matter in Parliament, which helped. After that our men were treated more like detainees than criminals. We were allowed visits, though only twice a week for half an hour each time.

○

We had no idea how long the men would be held. In a state of emergency, detention can be indefinite. In Alex's and Reg's case it ended up being five months and they were released in late August. Though we hoped for better, we were always ready for the long haul.

I went back and forth to the prison with fresh sets of clothes and food for Alex. Whenever possible we didn't let our men eat prison food. For Alex's birthday I brought chicken and potatoes and even strawberries and cream for dessert. I had to buy a lot because it wasn't meant only for Alex but for George Peake, Reg September, Barney Desai, my father-in-law Jimmy, and all the pals as well. When I handed the food in at the front desk, the sergeant demurred, 'We can't give him all this food. Where are we going to keep it?'

'Have you seen Alex?' I said. 'Have you seen his size? He's a tall, hefty man. He will finish the whole lot. You didn't say what we could or couldn't bring. I'm entitled to bring this food and he's entitled to have it.'

'But what prisoner can receive strawberries and cream?'

'This one can.'

A few years ago at the ninetieth birthday party of Sarah Carneson, I met an artist who had been detained with Alex at Roeland Street jail. He told me how they had all enjoyed the goodies that I brought Alex, including the strawberries and cream for his birthday. He remembered that the warders kept reminding the men that they were not at the Queen's banquet, but in prison.

○

One morning when we arrived at the jail, the door to the visiting area was closed. A policeman came round and told us there was no visiting that day because our white comrades had been shifted to Worcester a day earlier and black detainees would soon follow.

I just flew off the handle. I started banging on the thick wooden outside door, demanding my visit. I screamed and shouted and banged so hard that I hurt my wrist. The other women joined me.

Suddenly the prison superintendent appeared.

'We are entitled to a visit,' I told him. 'Come hell or high water, we will have that visit.'

'Let these bloody women in!' the superintendent told the guards. 'Give them just ten minutes. Those men are being moved today.'

We were allowed a ten-minute visit, instead of the thirty minutes to which we were entitled. As the men were being driven away in police vans, they sang freedom songs at the top of their voices. People passing in the street thought they were happy. But singing was a defence mechanism, not a sign of happiness. Who can be happy going to prison?

All of us women wanted to see our husbands that day at Worcester. We were entitled to another twenty minutes, and we were going to hold the authorities to that.

'Let's organise,' I said. 'If it means we have to hijack your car, then give it up. We're going to Worcester to see our men.'

Many people with cars rallied to our call, knowing that we couldn't pay for the journey. With some quick organisation we got to Worcester in time for the afternoon visit. When the men saw us they were taken aback: it was then that they realised we would not let anything happen to them.

○

For the next five months we visited the men in Worcester Prison regularly. Though some women didn't go every week, I did because I felt it was important. We travelled in a large convoy. White women whose husbands were detained took other wives in their cars. People from Langa and Nyanga hired buses. The women of the Black Sash also offered to drive us.* There was a real solidarity among the women across racial lines. We belonged to each other, and the children belonged to all of us.

To be on time for the morning visit at nine o'clock, we left Cape Town

---

* The Black Sash was a white women's resistance organisation founded in 1955. Black Sash members worked as volunteer advocates to families affected by apartheid laws, held street demonstrations, spoke at political meetings, brought cases of injustice to the attention of their MPs, and kept vigils outside Parliament and government offices, wearing distinctive black sashes as a mark of mourning.

by six, which meant we had to be up at five. Sometimes along the way a car would break down and we'd be stuck. If we missed our morning visit, we still had an afternoon visit, so we'd spend all day in Worcester waiting while the car was being repaired. When we got home finally at eleven, the children would be sleeping at a neighbour's house, just as we had left them hours earlier. We travelled in the dark both ways as it was winter. The route was dangerous, especially going over Du Toit's Kloof Pass. One chap who drove had a tendency to fall asleep: he suffered from a kind of sleeping sickness. Whenever I travelled in his car I sat perched on the seat next to him and watched his face. If he started to fall asleep I'd shake him awake. 'Look at the road!' Nothing, but nothing, could prevent us from seeing our men. It was our commitment not only to them, but to the whole struggle.

○

During all this time a coloured policeman, Mr Munnik, was good to us. He was a religious man who had joined the regular police force with the aim of helping stamp out crime. But after some time he was placed in the Special Branch. As he later told me, it was when he was given an order to raid the homes of decent people who had not committed any crimes that he realised what the real work of the Special Branch was. This went against his moral grain and really broke him. But he couldn't leave except by buying himself out of service, which cost too much.

Mr Munnik lived not far from us in Athlone. When he realised Alex had been arrested, he came to see me, making it look like he'd come to search the house. 'Mrs La Guma,' he said, 'please let me know if there's anything I can do to help.'

Before I accepted his offer, I asked my friend Ray Alexander, the trade union activist. Her husband Jack Simons was also detained during the State of Emergency, having been arrested at the University of Cape Town, where he lectured in politics. Ray said that if I was not offering bribes and Mr Munnik was not asking to be bribed, then she didn't see why Alex shouldn't receive gifts from me, using Mr Munnik as a go-between.

I then made small flat parcels of chicken, biltong, dried fruit and cigarettes which I discreetly gave Mr Munnik in the morning. It helped that he was a big, hefty man, because he could hide the parcel in the pocket of his jacket, although sometimes the poor packet was quite flattened as a result.

Alex always found a way to let me know he'd received the gifts. I'd sometimes send him smoked snoek, which Capetonians love. 'There's a new place selling some lovely smoked snoek,' I'd say. 'Yes, well it's a pity I can't get it, isn't it?' he'd reply. 'When I come out I'll get it.' In this way I knew he'd in fact got my parcel. I'd say, 'Well, I'm trying to give up smoking you know.' If Alex joked, 'Yes, that's why I'm smoking more,' I'd know he'd received the cigarettes. We had to manoeuvre verbally so that anybody listening didn't catch on.

All these little things helped the men see that we were trying to do all we could for them. Mr Munnik never asked for anything in return and I never offered. He was later able to buy his way out of the Special Branch. He then became a marked man as the authorities realised he was on our side, supporting people whom he arrested and whose houses he had previously raided. But he wasn't caught out.

During apartheid we never knew all the risks we ran. One either took chances opposing apartheid or did nothing and lived under its misery. My comrades and I preferred to take the risks.

○

When Alex was arrested, he'd been working on his first novel, *A Walk in the Night*. I don't know how long he'd been writing or how much more he had to write. He never told me, and I never asked. When I found him busy, I'd say, 'Can I start typing?' 'No, leave it,' because it wasn't time. But when he was in Worcester jail he asked me to find the written manuscript, proofread it, and post it to Ulli Beier at Mbari Publications in Ibadan, Nigeria.

I looked in all the places I could think of and eventually found the manuscript at home, hidden under a file of loose papers. Everything had to be hidden, because when the Special Branch raided the house they took everything away. Quite often when Alex started to write something, they'd arrive in a raid and take it away; then he had to start again. In some cases his books were published years apart because, in addition to being a meticulous writer, he had his papers taken away before he could continue.

I proofread the handwritten manuscript and made my corrections in black ink. There was only one manuscript, but what could I do? There was no time to make copies or write out a second copy. I just thought, 'Get it away.' I wrapped up the copy neatly and posted it off.

When the State of Emergency ended and Alex came out of detention in August 1960, Ulli had not yet replied to say that he'd received the book. Fortunately, I had registered the book in the post. I took the certificate back to the Athlone post office and told them that it hadn't been received. The official said he would investigate the matter. About two weeks later the book arrived at our house: it had never been posted. When we got it back I was ready to send it again. But then something unexpected happened: Ulli Beier showed up on our doorstep.

He must have realised something was holding up the work, knowing what the circumstances were like in South Africa. So while he was in Cape Town he made a point of seeing Alex – even coming to our house and asking me where he could find him. By this time Alex was back at *New Age*. But things were so terrible in the country that I couldn't just give Alex's whereabouts to a man whom I'd never met before. So I lied. 'I don't know where he is. He hasn't come home yet and I don't really know when he'll be home.'

Ulli must have known I was trying to protect Alex. He realised Alex wasn't in Jo'burg or detained, so he went to the *New Age* office and found him there.

At five o'clock Alex walked through the door. I was about to tell him that Ulli had visited, but then Ulli stepped in right behind him. I was so embarrassed I didn't know where to hide my face.

'You did the right thing,' Alex said. Then he turned to Ulli, 'This is how we have to operate here. We don't give information to anybody we don't know. It's quite normal.'

Alex gave the manuscript to Ulli, who took it back to Nigeria. They typeset it, printed it and launched it there. Ulli kept the original manuscript.

When I first read *A Walk in the Night*, I could place almost every one of the characters in the book. His descriptions are wonderful. Living in my community I was able to recognise the people and places he describes in District Six. When he writes about a cockroach, you can almost see it coming through the crack in the wall. 'Yes,' I thought, 'this *is* District Six.'

When Alex was banned in July 1961 none of his writing or spoken words could be quoted. The newspapers couldn't print anything about Alex as a banned person. That's why when the novel was published in 1962, the headline in the *Cape Argus* said in bold type, 'Too Hot to Hold.'

Alex was often at his typewriter, but I never knew when he was working on a book since he also wrote articles for *New Age*. I only learned he was working on *A Walk in the Night* when he asked me to read part of a draft. Once when I thought I should start typing, he tore up the pages because he was not happy with them. He probably started on the novel earlier than 1959. He was meticulous and took a long time to write. The book had only 90 pages, though I think he intended to put in more. The writer and critic Lewis Nkosi once said that Alex achieved in 90 pages what other writers could not achieve in a much longer book.

Chapter 12

'We knew this meant that some would die'

In late March 1961, Nelson Mandela called a three-day general strike to protest against South Africa becoming a republic on 31 May. We knew that if this happened, things would get even worse under the Nats. To launch the anti-Republic campaign political activists like Alex went underground to distribute leaflets and encourage the strike. Even before he became a noted writer Alex was well known for his political activities. His name appeared in the papers as a Treason Trialist and political activist detained during the 1960 State of Emergency. Now, like others, he went into hiding and did his political work at night to avoid arrest and detention.

While I remained with the children at our house in Garlandale, I found safe houses for Alex during the campaign. These were in Athlone where he was working to mobilise forces for the strike. When I took him to a safe house we often walked openly in the streets because it was safer that way. He strode next to me while I did my midwifery rounds in my nurse's uniform with my delivery bag, as if he were the 'father' of the baby I was going to deliver. At other times *he* was the 'baby' I visited. I went to see if there was anything he wanted and I told him what was happening on the outside.

Sometimes I used my delivery bag to carry political leaflets in a way that couldn't be discovered by the Special Branch. I had two delivery bags, both kept as sterile as possible. The upper compartment of the bags contained the sterile equipment such as stainless steel bowls, forceps and scissors. In the lower compartment I kept unsterile equipment, like my plastic apron and rubber mattress cover. When the need arose, which was fairly often, I stuffed as many leaflets as I could, neatly folded, into the lower compartment between the folds of the apron and mattress cover. I also stuffed leaflets into little sterile bags and flattened them against the sides of the lining so that the bag didn't seem bulky. I always allowed the Special Branch to search my bag, although I told them firmly that if a patient of mine died because of their germs I would sue them. I was never caught. After the search, I'd again sterilise the bag and its contents in case I had two calls in quick succession.

◕

Once I had a scare when Spyker van Wyk came to our house with another member of the Special Branch. They wanted to know where Alex was.

'Alex isn't here,' I said. 'He's left me.' I wanted to throw them off the scent.

'You see what these men do to you,' Van Wyk said. 'You have them as husbands and have two children by them and they just leave you. Tell us if he's out with another woman.'

'Well, I don't know,' I said, playing innocent. He didn't know that I was the one hiding Alex.

During this time I also received threatening phone calls. The callers, all men, phoned around midnight. 'We have just killed your husband,' one said. A few days later another said, 'We have just killed your husband.'

'Oh really?' I answered. 'For a *second* time?'

I wasn't intimidated by these calls. I knew they were trying to frighten me, but by then I'd been hardened and didn't believe a word they said. When they phoned me a third time to tell me they'd killed Alex, I said, 'Where can I find the body?' I didn't get any more calls after that.

One night I was awakened by the phone. The man on the other end said: 'Tell your husband to watch his step. We are going to get him. You won't see him alive after tonight.' Speaking in a deep voice and rolling his *r*'s, he added: 'This is the Supreme Commander of the Ku Klux Klan.'

Later that night while the children and I were in bed, I heard a *crash-bang-clatter*. I was petrified. I knew that petrol bombs had recently been thrown through the windows of others in the movement, so my first thought was to get the children out. Eugene (then five) and Barto (then two) were already wide awake and trembling. I got them up and into our room. I looked out and caught a glimpse of someone jumping onto the running board of the car as it drove off, but I couldn't see the number because Garlandale still had no streetlights. We heard the car speeding away with the culprits – no doubt the security police.

By that time my neighbours Mrs Zinn and Mrs Dixon had thrown open their doors and come over straight away because they knew we were being attacked. I said to the boys, 'Mommy's going to put you through the window and Mrs Zinn will take you. Sit here, Eugene. Let Mommy first get Barto out. Barto is small.'

I lifted Barto and then Eugene through a bedroom window and Mrs Zinn received them on the other side. I didn't pass them through the front door because that's where I thought the bomb had fallen and where the next shot would be fired.

I quickly went back to the front room to find out how much of the house was on fire. It was then that I discovered that it wasn't a petrol bomb but rather a huge stone that had been thrown through the window. It must have taken two men to throw it.

Mrs Dixon's teenage boys John and Winnie came over as did Mrs Zinn's son Dudley, a young man who was very fond of Alex.

'We're staying over, Nurse,' one of the boys said. 'If they come again God help them, because we're going to work their case for them. Let them come!'

The boys said they wanted to take my place.

'Like hell,' I said. 'I am *not* moving out of this house!'

In fact, I was petrified. Though I didn't know what was happening, I was determined not to move out. If I did, the Special Branch would have won.

I never felt fear as I did that night. But for my children's sake I pretended to be brave. The telephone rang. It was the *Cape Times*, phoning to see if I was all right. I asked how they knew there had been an incident. They said they'd received a call from Lulu Peake, wife of

George Peake, who was in the Coloured People's Congress (CPC) and, like Alex, working underground in the campaign against the Republic.* She'd also had a huge stone – really a boulder, as she put it – thrown through her window. Lulu was wise to have called the press. The *Cape Times* thought to phone me because they knew Alex would inevitably be targeted.

My neighbours felt tremendously angry. They had the greatest respect for us, and even though they didn't take part in the struggle as deeply as Alex and I did, they supported us. Eugene and Barto stayed the night at Mrs Dixon's, and the Dixon and Zinn boys guarded the house. This was the true community spirit, the feeling that if you needed help, people were there to help you.

The next morning I went to see Alex at his safe house. I always tried to be cheerful and keep up his spirits. But he saw my face was ashen and asked what had happened. After I told him he said, 'Well, this is the kind of thing we must expect. Just stay indoors and fortify the place. Try to guard the house as best you can.'

I reported the matter to the Athlone police that morning, as my calls to them the previous night hadn't got through. I told *New Age*, 'We refuse to be intimidated. I have every confidence in the political work in which my husband is engaged, and we will not be intimidated by pro-government hooligans.'

We didn't move out; we stayed. They were trying to frighten us, to get us to shut up, to stop telling people not to support us. But we weren't about to change a thing we were doing. We acted in total, continual, and undeterred defiance.

After the anti-Republic campaign ended, Alex was arrested on his way to work. Both he and Reg September, then general secretary of the CPC, served twelve days in Pollsmoor, where Mandela was later detained. When Alex and Reg were about to be released, their detention

---

* George Peake was a founding member, with Reg September, of the South African Coloured People's Organisation, later the Coloured People's Congress (CPC). It was Peake who greeted Mandela, Sisulu, Ahmed Kathrada and Govan Mbeki when they arrived on Robben Island in 1964. Peake had been sentenced to three years for planting explosives outside Roeland Street jail.

was extended by another twelve days. Hettie and I visited them at Pollsmoor and brought them food. The regime was already beginning its detention-without-trial system: in 1963 detention in solitary confinement was introduced by law for up to 90 days.

◯

One Friday in July 1961 Reg September came to the house and told me I'd be making a journey that evening outside Cape Town.

'Pack your bags. Be ready by five o'clock,' he said. 'Only we two will know about this.'

I was going to a political meeting in Durban and it had to be kept secret. When Alex came home that evening and found me with a little bag packed, ready to go, he said jokingly, 'So you're leaving me!'

'No, only temporarily, for the weekend,' I said. 'I've been told to go away, and a car will fetch me at five o'clock.' I said nothing more.

I had been chosen to go to the meeting as a delegate of the CPC, along with my comrades Sam Kahn, Ronnie Hendricks and Cardiff Marney, who drove his car. Though Reg and Alex were in the top echelons of the CPC in Cape Town, they didn't go because Alex, and perhaps Reg also, had either just been banned or sensed they were about to be banned. But I'd also played a political role, so I suppose the leadership felt I could be part of this important meeting. It turned out to be a major historical event: it involved the decision of the ANC and its allies to take up the armed struggle.

We drove through the night and arrived the next day. It was winter time and freezing. The frost iced up the windscreen and every now and then we'd have to get out and wipe it down quickly with warm water.

It was important that we not make ourselves visible, so we had sandwiches and tea and coffee from flasks in the car. I sat with Ronnie in the back while Sam sat with Cardiff up front. I cuddled up close to Ronnie to keep warm. There was nothing wrong with this. We needed each other's body heat and it was better for us to sit together than for him to be on one side of the car and me on the other. We trusted ourselves. We were comrades, closer than brother and sister or even husband and wife.

When we arrived in Durban on Saturday morning, we were greeted by Billy Nair. Billy was a trade unionist and longtime member of the Natal Indian Congress. He later served twenty years on Robben Island for sabotage as a member of Umkhonto we Sizwe. When they released him, he didn't want to walk out without his friends who were still inside.*

That night we drove out into the countryside where the meeting was held in a huge building. As the ANC had been banned since the 1960 State of Emergency, we had to meet clandestinely. It was like a cave inside, dimly lit with candles. There were fewer than fifty of us there from the ANC and other organisations of the Congress Alliance from the various provinces.

Walter Sisulu, Govan Mbeki and Nelson Mandela were among those present. At that time Nelson was travelling around the country, building support for the movement. It was wonderful to be among them. We realised how honoured we were to be at this historic meeting with high-profile members of the ANC and with Chief Albert Luthuli in the chair. I had met Chief previously when he toured South Africa. Zollie Malindi, chairman of the ANC in the Western Cape, and Jimmy La Guma, then president of the CPC, had arranged the Chief's tour in Cape Town. He drew crowds of people, filling every square metre of space in the meeting halls. Cape Town coloureds were not accustomed to going to such political rallies, so it was wonderful that they turned out in vast numbers to support him.

At the meeting that night there was great debate and conflict over the question of armed struggle. Nelson was in favour of armed struggle, whereas Chief Luthuli was known for trying to bring about change through peaceful protest. In December he would win the Nobel Peace Prize. It was difficult to ask Chief to support the armed struggle, but it was critical to get his approval.

The Chief sat listening, giving everybody a fair chance to speak. When the debate was exhausted, the hall grew quiet.

---

* A veteran anti-apartheid activist, Nair was held in the same section of Robben Island Prison as Nelson Mandela and the other Rivonia Trialists. After his release from prison in 1984, Nair became a leading activist in the United Democratic Front and an ANC MP from 1994 to 1999.

There he sat. We were all on tenterhooks. 'Is he going to say yes? What is he going to say?' We knew we couldn't make any move without Chief Luthuli announcing whether he approved of armed struggle.

Chief placed one hand over the other beneath his chin and in his dignified, soft, clear, firm voice said: 'Since we have tried all peaceful methods of attempting to gain our liberation from oppression, the time has come for us to try other methods.'

I wept. The tension was broken and the tears just rolled. The Chief had given his blessing to the armed struggle. I cried when this enormous decision had been made that would lead us into the future.*

That night the four of us went back to Billy Nair's house and slept a bit before making our way home on Sunday. When I got back to Cape Town I couldn't keep the news from Alex because it was already out. Alex gave a big smile. He just grinned with his whole mouth. 'The old man said yes.'

We were going to start a guerrilla war from scratch. We knew this meant that some would die. But we also knew that you either go for it and take whatever is going to come, or you sit and do nothing and things just keep getting worse. One way or another you might get killed by the Special Branch. Look at all the torture that followed. Look at how many people were taken, shot, interrogated or thrown down ten stories. This was a hard decision, given what might happen in an armed struggle. But we had to do something to bring about change, even if it carried a heavy sacrifice.

People focused on the 1970s and 1980s as the years of struggle against apartheid. Certainly those years are important. But what many don't realise is that the 1970s and 1980s were built on the pillars of the 1950s and 1960s.

---

* The decision to take up the armed struggle occurred over two nights in July 1961 in Stanger, north of Durban, at the farmhouse of an Indian sugar plantation owner, so that Chief Luthuli, who had been banished to his farm nearby, could participate. Luthuli, who was morally committed to non-violence, was persuaded by the rhetoric of Mandela and others that armed struggle was necessary. After an initial meeting of the ANC National Executive Committee, the full assembly authorised Mandela to form a new military organisation, separate from the ANC, which would come to be known as Umkhonto we Sizwe or MK (Spear of the Nation).

Veterans of the struggle reunite: Wolfie Kodesh, Denis Goldberg, Blanche and Albie Sachs

Chapter 13

'I grabbed hold of Govan and began hugging and kissing him'

In that same month, July 1961, the state imposed a five-year banning order on Reg September and Alex. More than two thousand people came to an open-air meeting to protest against their bannings. Not content simply to ban Alex, eighteen months later the regime placed Alex under house arrest in December 1962.

That day Alex and I had gone into town to buy Christmas presents for the boys. When we returned home two Special Branch men, Mr Genis and Mr Van Wyk, were waiting to give Alex the house arrest order. They had been put in charge of watching Alex. Whenever they came to the house after that, the two of them were always together. Later, when they bullied Eugene at school, it was the same two – always Genis and Van Wyk.*

Genis said to Alex: 'I've been given a job to look after you, and I do my job very well.'

Alex replied: 'Yes, Mr Genis, I also have been given a job to do, and I also do my job very well.'

I knew what house arrest was going to do to Alex, a vibrant young man who was politically active. When the children came home from school I said to them, 'It's sad, but Daddy has been placed under house arrest.' Eugene's face just fell. But Barto jumped up and down. 'Ooh! Now my

---

* Lieutenant (later Major) Dirk Kotze Genis and Sergeant Andries van Wyk were assigned to watch and torment the La Guma family. According to the TRC, Genis was one of at least seven security policemen who received special training in torture techniques in France and Algeria in the early 1960s. Genis and Van Wyk were the officers responsible for the interrogation of Imam Haron from May to September 1969 when he was found dead in his cell.

Daddy won't go to prison anymore.' House arrest for him meant that when he came home from school, his Daddy would be there. Little did Barto know what was waiting for him, for the next year Alex and I would both be arrested. But for now, Daddy was home and that was all that mattered.

Of the three restrictions the state could impose on individuals – banning, house arrest or banishment – to my mind banishment was the worst.[*] So I satisfied myself that although house arrest was terrible, it was better than Alex being banished to a strange, distant, isolated part of South Africa. In the course of things, however, house arrest nearly drove him to destruction.

◯

In 1962 and 1963, some of the top brass of the ANC High Command came down from Jo'burg and it was my job to find safe houses for them. Govan Mbeki, father of Thabo Mbeki, was one of them.[†] Govan sometimes came to our house while Alex was under house arrest and not allowed to see anybody except his mother, my parents, a doctor or lawyer who was not banned, and me. It was a big risk coming to see us.

Once Govan arrived unexpectedly in a taxi. Eugene, who was playing outside, ran in and announced, 'Mommy, Uncle Govan is here.' Govan followed Eugene inside as if it were perfectly normal. I was shivering in my boots, wondering where I was going to take Govan. Since I didn't have a car at the time we had to walk to the safe house. On our way we passed a railway line just as the train was pulling into Athlone station at peak hour, full of people arriving home from work. I turned and saw a police van right behind us. I didn't know if it was following us. I grabbed hold of Govan and began hugging and kissing him.

---

[*]   In response to mass action campaigns in the early 1960s, the apartheid regime stepped up its crackdown through amendments to the Suppression of Communism Act of 1950 that provided for the banning, house arrest or banishment of any person publicly opposed to the state. By the end of 1964, at least 350 people had been banned, and 48, including Alex La Guma, were placed under house arrest.

[†]   Govan Mbeki (1910-2001) became deeply involved in ANC politics in Port Elizabeth, a centre of ANC activity. In 1963 he went underground to join Umkhonto we Sizwe, the armed wing of the ANC. In 1964 he was arrested for treason and sentenced to life imprisonment on Robben Island along with Nelson Mandela and other ANC leaders.

Govan didn't know what to do. 'Blanche,' he said. 'What's happening?'
'Just hold me tight,' I said. 'Kiss me and hold me tight.'

As we stood holding each other, the train lurched past and some male passengers whistled and shouted just as they would when they saw any couple kissing. I turned my face to see the police van behind us, and when it drove past Govan realised what it was all about.

Poor Govan! I can still picture his face. He was more shocked than surprised when I wrapped my arms around him. It wasn't a long passionate kiss, just a peck on the cheek. But perhaps because of our embrace he was able to avoid arrest and do his work in Cape Town before going back to Jo'burg.

When I returned home, Alex said he was relieved to see me because the police had been to our house. I could only think they must have been connected with the police van that had passed us in the street.

○

One day I walked into the house and saw Walter Sisulu lying on the bed quite comfortably. He knew very well that he had no right to be there – not because he wasn't welcome, but because it was dangerous.

'Walter! What are you doing here?'

'Blanche, don't you want me here?'

'Oh for goodness' sake, Walter, I didn't say what I meant. But we'll have to get you out of here quickly.'

'Yes, I know that,' he said calmly. Then I took him to a safe house.

At another time Raymond Mhlaba came to Cape Town.* I didn't know it at the time, but members of the ANC executive including Nelson Mandela and Walter Sisulu were working clandestinely at Lilliesleaf Farm in Rivonia outside Johannesburg. When they came unexpectedly to Cape Town, I was one of the people responsible for finding safe houses. I'd made plans in advance and took Raymond to my parents' house, having told my mother, but not my father, who Raymond

---

* Raymond Mhlaba (1920–2005) was a key ANC leader who joined the Communist Party and became secretary for the Port Elizabeth branch until the party was banned. In 1961 Mhlaba went into exile for military training and on his return in 1962 commanded Umkhonto we Sizwe until his arrest in 1963 at Rivonia and subsequent imprisonment on Robben Island.

was. Frankly, my mother could keep a secret better than my father. He was inclined unwittingly to let friends know what he'd been told, which could be dangerous because the security police were waiting for just this information.

Raymond had come to Cape Town dressed as a priest, wearing a white dog collar. A day or two after I left Raymond with my parents, my father came to our house and said to me, 'You know, I think there's a problem. I think that guy is a spy.'

'But how do you know?'

'Well, he's supposed to be a priest but he doesn't know how to wear the collar. Why is that?'

I thought quickly and said, 'Look, Dad, he's *learning* to be a priest. He's come out here to do fieldwork. And since you know how to pin the collar because your father was a priest, perhaps you can help him.'

'Oh, then that's all right,' my Dad said. Then quite proudly: 'I just thought I should tell you, because I must protect all of you people.'

I didn't often have to lie to my own father and I tried to avoid it. In the circumstances of Struggle your values shift. Lying to my father wasn't as important as being loyal to the Movement. After all, we were operating in a world where the whole apartheid system was a lie. By telling the truth I could have said something that might lead to Raymond's arrest, and under torture he might have revealed the names of others in the High Command at Rivonia. As it was, they were arrested in July 1963 and tried for sabotage. Loyalty was more necessary than the truth.

○

Within the Movement we all had to take on the role of public speaking at some stage. Alex and Reg were always the ones asked to speak. But when Alex was banned I was suddenly told one morning, 'You'll have to speak at a meeting this afternoon on the Grand Parade.' What a shock!

Standing in front of the crowd on the Grand Parade it felt like my heart was travelling up and down to my feet and back. I said to Denis Goldberg's wife, Esmé, who was standing beside me, 'I don't know what I'm going to say!' When I spoke I must have said the right thing because people applauded. The minute I finished, Esmé, who was a physiotherapist, started to massage me. Somebody else came and shoved a pill in my mouth – it was a Disprin. I must have been in quite a state.

I subsequently learned how to speak in public from Albie Sachs. We were informed that whoever wanted to practise public speaking could pitch up at a certain Party member's house on Sunday morning to learn from Albie. There were ten or twelve of us at the first meeting. Albie started off by saying, 'Explain how you would fry an egg. Start with the utensils that you need. Put it all out. How you are going to open that egg? How are you going to serve it?'

Then we'd get up and have our say and he'd criticise our little speeches. 'You left out so-and-so. And what did you cook with? You didn't tell us that you had a pan to cook in.' That was his way of teaching us. He was tremendous, an important person not only to me, but to many of us. I carry Albie in high esteem still today, and not just because he's a judge. Albie is a thoroughly good person – an ordinary, good person, a kind, upstanding man.

Once I was told at the last minute that I had to chair an ANC meeting because Alex was unable to attend. 'Oh my God,' I thought. I was still learning, and I'd never been asked to lead a big meeting. Kenny Parker, a friend and a member of the Coloured People's Congress (CPC), came with me and spoke as well. When we were heckled and shouted down by some people from the Unity Movement, Kenny tried to protect me. 'Madam Chair,' he said, 'they don't even respect you as a woman.'

As they wouldn't let us speak, we had to close the meeting.

Unfortunately, the Unity Movement fought the Congress Movement harder than they fought the regime. They were wreckers out to disrupt our meetings. It was especially bad in the Cape, where the Unity Movement placed anti-Congress articles in the newspapers and heckled our speakers. They were against apartheid, but they didn't actually fight apartheid – they fought *us*, putting their energies against us because they wouldn't risk fighting the regime. Their organisation consisted mostly of teachers and doctors and other members of the professional class. Since teachers were employed by the apartheid regime, they had to think of their salaries. Thus, the Unity Movement's main and sometimes only form of protest was to boycott everything, which required little risk. Though some of their people were banned, none went to prison and none of them suffered the ultimate – solitary confinement. A doctor whom I once challenged said to me, 'We cannot bite the hand that feeds us.' People like that would never have won the battle, even partially. We too had families but we took chances, regardless of the consequences. Consider how Alex gave up everything, as did so many others. Like the workers we felt we had nothing to lose but our chains. The Unity Movement *said* they 'opposed' the regime. Well, we *fought* it.*

○

Even with all the restrictions, Alex and I were able to do political work. We worked for the Coloured People's Congress under the banner of the banned ANC. Our task was to mobilise the coloured people. The whites did the same in the Congress of Democrats and the Indians in the Indian Congress. We all worked under the banner of the ANC. It was well co-ordinated. You wouldn't get a CPC person saying something different from an ANC person.

Alex was a top man in the Movement, writing documents to different branches in places like Paarl, Wellington, Worcester and Robinson. He analysed the political situation and presented a method of action, informing all the members what to do so that our work was co-ordinated.

We worked at night, with black curtains drawn and the room lit only by small candles. We'd write the documents while sitting on our haunches or lying on the floor so that if there was a knock at the door we could make everything disappear quickly. We'd then answer the door in our nightgowns as if we'd been sleeping.

I was twice a member of Communist Party cells. First I was placed in a cell with Sarah Carneson and Ruth Gottschalk. We would meet

---

* The Non-European Unity Movement (NEUM), formed in 1943 and designated as the Unity Movement in 1964, emphasised equality of the franchise, civil liberties, free education and redistribution of land. Though open to all, the Unity Movement consisted mainly of coloured professionals in the Cape such as teachers, lawyers and doctors. Its reluctance to engage in mass action brought the scorn of the ANC and the Communist Party, its rivals for popular support.

at Sarah's house, where we discussed papers she'd received from the Central Committee and agree what our next tasks were. Then I was placed into a cell with Denis Goldberg, Liz Abrahams and Ilse Fischer. Denis was the only white person who was caught at Rivonia and served 21 years in Pretoria Central Prison.

If Alex was at home, I'd leave the children with him. Otherwise I'd take them to my mother or they'd stay with Mrs Dixon next door. I'd tell both my mother and the boys, 'I'm just going out to see a patient.' I had to tell a lot of lies, unfortunately. As much as I tried to be honest and truthful, I couldn't always do it. We were dealing with a dishonest regime, so to lie by saying that I was going 'there' when I was really going 'here' didn't hurt my conscience at all. It was either tell that lie or get out of the Movement. We couldn't jeopardise other people's positions because we were trying to be 'good'.

Working in the second cell with Denis was dangerous. As all of us were banned we couldn't meet just anywhere, so we met in Denis's car. We'd synchronise our watches and arrive clandestinely at a predetermined place. We couldn't be a minute early or a second late, because that minute or second could be the end of us. We came on the dot, left, and that was it. It was a matter of disciplined people working together in unison.

We often met near the Rondebosch Common or else near Rhodes Memorial at night, about halfway up because it was dark. As I didn't have a car I'd take a bus to Mowbray and walk. Years later Denis said to me, 'Blanche, I was looking at that road the other day. You know, I never realised you walked up that road alone.' We'd stay and sit together, using a pencil torchlight to read documents on the floor of Denis's car. The document would be a short directive – what the next move was, what to expect. We'd make quick work of it, then be gone.

We also distributed leaflets at night. The leaflets encouraged people not to accept apartheid, but to mount peaceful protests, organised by the Movement. We worked late at night when there were few people out, disposing of the leaflets through letter boxes or by throwing them into the gardens of houses. For our own security we did not hand out leaflets to people on the street.

One night we went all the way out to Paarl. After distributing as many leaflets as we could, we had to get home but there were still many leaflets left over. We couldn't be caught with them, so we left them at the bus stop for the southeaster wind to blow to areas we couldn't reach. What better way to distribute them?

None of us could have done this work alone. We were committed at any cost to bringing about change in the country. And we were disciplined: when given a task we did it, and we didn't ask questions. I became so oriented to a task that it filled my whole being.

Everything depended on an enormous level of trust. We trusted the people at the top to know what they were doing. And we trusted everybody within our circle. That trust was as profound as the level of trust in a good marriage. I never felt that trust betrayed.

○

I often said to the children, 'Twenty-four hours isn't enough.' I had to see to so many things that I could never finish a day's work unless I worked late into the night or even into early the next morning. I had to see Alex while he was in prison; I had to see my patients; I had to see to my children; and I had to attend to my daily chores. I couldn't afford to pay somebody to do them for me. When he was older, Barto said to me, 'Yes Mum, and if you had forty-eight hours, even that wouldn't be enough.' There was just too much to do.

I was always exhausted. I felt that sitting down to have a cup of tea was wasting time. I should have slept more, I was so tired. I was mentally exhausted as well, worrying about Alex, especially when he was in prison. My mind would race, wondering what would happen to him and to us. Day after day, week after week, year after year, I felt like a zombie walking around, doing what I had to do to keep the wolf from the door. I often didn't have enough money to feed the family. When I had the rare good month – that is, when some of my patients paid me – I could pay the electricity and the rates in advance. When the next month brought in little, then at least the bills had been paid and I didn't have to worry about them.

Finally, the exhaustion got to me. Once when I was leaving a Party meeting at Sarah Carneson's house, her husband Fred saw me and said, 'God, but you're dying on your feet. You're ill. And last time I saw you, you were also ill.'

I was in fact ill with a bad case of bronchitis. It was winter and I had got wet and caught a chest infection. It occurred every time I attended cell meetings in winter. But my commitment to the Party and to the country meant that I didn't stay at home and make excuses not to attend. So I went, even though I knew I was not well.

Fred decided that I needed a car and took me with him to look at second-hand cars. 'What can you pay towards the car?' he asked. What a question! I was the only one working in our family, and I had no money at all. Though I didn't get a car then, I was given one in August 1964 after my detention.

I first found out about the car when Eugene and Barto returned from a birthday party for Rita Tabakin's son. My friend Nancy Dick took them to the party because I was banned. Coming home, the boys brought a cake for me from Rita. On the box was written, 'August 1st.' As Eugene explained, Rita had said I was going to get a car on 1 August (1964).

'Just hold on Eugene!' Barto interrupted. 'Mommy, there's something more. You're going to get a brand-new car out of the box.' Then he looked at me. 'Mommy, just how *big* is the box?'

I didn't know who gave me the car, and I still don't know, though I learned later that Rita was one of the donors. But the seed for that car was planted at the meetings I attended in Fred Carneson's house. It was through his effort that friends pulled together to get the car. They also paid for driving lessons and my licence. I never learned who they were, because when I wanted to thank them, my lawyer Himie Bernadt said, 'No, they know. I will thank them for you.'

In fact, because Himie arranged the purchase of the car, the security police raided his offices, hoping to find out who had provided the money. Every move we made was monitored. With Alex under house arrest and me a midwife earning little, they suspected that Party members had given us the car at a time when the Communist Party was banned. There was nothing illegal about the transaction at all. In any case, the Communist Party couldn't have given the car. Like us, the Party was too poor.

The car, a pale blue Ford Anglia four-seater, was a tremendous help. My practice grew because I could get to my patients more easily. Previously I'd ridden my motorised bicycle. Now I could travel in the rain without catching cold. Having a car meant an end to the days when people saw me on my bike with my nurse's cape flying and thought of me as Batman.

As Alex never learned how to drive and always took public transport, the only time he even rode in the car was when I once took him to a court appointment. Being a new driver, I got stuck on a hill. At the top of the hill I had to make a sharp turn to the left, and couldn't get the jolly thing to move. Alex had to be in court at nine o'clock and time was marching on. I looked across the road and saw a traffic officer.

'Officer!' I yelled.

'Yes.'

'She's just giving a spot of bother this morning and I can't get her to go,' I said.

'Oh fine,' he said. He got into the car and took it round the corner.

'Thank you very much.' I said.

'Lovely new car,' he said.

'Thank you, officer. You drive well, too.'

He just laughed. 'No,' he said. 'You needed help and you asked for help, and we got it through.'

He certainly didn't know whom he was assisting that morning.

Chapter 14

'And that's when the words hit me: Don't betray'

It was a day in October 1963 just like any other. The air was chilly and we began the day with breakfast and getting the children ready for school. Alex had been under house arrest for almost a year. After taking the children to school I set out on my nursing round. I had midwifery patients all over Athlone so I was on my bike by eight o'clock to visit all the mothers and babies. When I came back to our house around eleven, I saw several cars and three or four huge police vans parked outside. I thought, 'There's a raid.'

I didn't know just how massive a raid it would be. Previously our two Special Branch men, Genis and Van Wyk, came and scratched around a bit. But when I went inside this time, the place was teeming with men. About ten policemen in suits were turning the whole house upside down, looking inside and behind the cupboards, upsetting mattresses and looking under the beds, tearing apart the stitching on the furniture and cutting open the backs of chairs. They had taken the soiled washing, turned the pockets inside out and gone through my clothes, particularly my underwear. They were cutting open my sanitary pads.

'Is everything all right?' I asked Alex.

'How can everything be all right?' he said. 'Just look at it. Look at the mess this place is in.'

I didn't know what to say. When I walked in and found my home like this, it really knocked me off my balance.

The Special Branch were looking for documents. They thought we were trying to overthrow the government and they were right – though not through sabotage, but with ideas. They knew we didn't have guns.

Alex and I weren't entirely surprised because we'd been raided several times before, usually at two or three in the morning. We understood the consequences of our politics. We knew the stress of the security police coming to the house, arresting Alex, even threatening to kidnap our children. So the raid was nothing new. But this time there were so many of them and they really turned the house upside down, even opening the trap door to see if we had anything hidden in the ceiling.

One of the things they found was a midwifery textbook. They had a good laugh at the drawing of a woman lying naked while giving birth. 'They're warped,' I thought. They were more to be pitied than blamed.

I also had a box in which I kept my midwifery register. I had to keep the records of every patient – what happened, how it happened, and whether there was any abnormality. The supervisor of midwives came around periodically to check the register and see that I was doing my work properly. These Special Branch men opened this register and saw the initials ANC.

'Look!' they said. 'She's one of them. Told you this girl was a communist. Says here she's ANC.'

'No,' I said. 'That's Ante-Natal Clinic.'

'You could tell us anything,' they said. 'This is ANC! It says ANC!'

But of course they knew it wasn't. They could see that the register related to my patients.

'It's confidential,' I said.

'Ah Blanche, nothing about your life is confidential.'

Then they took out big woven bags of thick hessian cloth used for rough type of work. They packed about eight of the bags with all of our books, including the works of Marx, Engels and Lenin, which were banned. Everything went, including Alex's writing. These raids really frustrated him. Every time the Special Branch came, they took away all his writing.

'What's happening?' I asked Alex as I watched them tear apart my house.

'Just take it easy,' he said, trying to calm me.

I thought to myself, 'I'm better off if I do something like making breakfast.' So I made Alex some breakfast – scrambled eggs and bacon.

I wanted to make these policemen smell the lovely bacon and be jealous. Before they hauled him away, Alex had his full breakfast. It was almost like the Last Supper.

'Alex, we're taking you,' they said.

But just as they were taking him, Van Wyk said to me, 'Blanche, jy ook.' (You also.)

I was shocked. I had no idea I was going to be arrested. It had never happened before.

Alex was always the one taken, not me.

My mind was already in a state from seeing what they had done to my house. Now I thought, 'What about Eugene and Barto when they come home?' I also had all of my patients to think about.

I told them, 'I've got to write up all the cases I'm expected to attend because I'm booked three months in advance. The women are due to have their babies by then.' I then wrote down all the names and addresses of my patients and the amount of the deposits they had made because my supervisor had to know. Most of the women paid me a fee ahead of time. But to be sure that I never touched this money since it wasn't yet mine, I put it into the bank. In fact, the *only* money I had in the bank was these people's deposits. I then phoned my supervisor, a white woman. 'Mrs Billis, I'm being arrested. It's a political arrest,' I said. 'I'm being taken away. They're giving you ten minutes and, in case you don't get here in time, the money in the bank belongs to the patients. Make it clear that if other nurses take over my work then the money is to be given to them.'

The Special Branch men timed Mrs Billis coming from town. She made it just in time to see me being taken away. All I could think was, 'My children! My children! What about the children?'

After we left, Alex's mother cleaned up the mess and when the children came home from school she explained to them what happened. One neighbour told me later that Eugene was in tears. We had hidden some of Alex's books and documents under Eugene's bed. This was Eugene's special responsibility – to look after Daddy's things. When he came home from school that day, the first thing he did was look under his mattress and see the books were missing. 'Oh, they've taken my

Daddy!' he said and then started crying. He felt he had failed his Dad by not looking well enough after his things.

○

Alex and I sat in the back of the sedan with two Special Branch men in front. They had put us together, hoping to hear what we had to say to each other. We said nothing. We knew we were being detained, and talking would just have made things worse.

I said to him, whispering and gesticulating, 'Why did they arrest me? What have *I* done wrong?'

'What do you think?' he said. 'We are both fighting against apartheid. That is a crime. Stop being so naïve.'

I am a naïve person. But I can only think my arrest was sheer vindictiveness on the part of the Special Branch. I was certainly involved in the Struggle; I did deliver leaflets and provide safe houses. In fact, I don't think they knew how deeply I *was* involved in the Communist Party. But they were really after Alex.

Before we arrived at the prison Alex turned to me and whispered, 'Say nothing!'

○

They threw us into the police station at Maitland, and there we were separated. None of those who were detained were sent to the big prisons. The Special Branch just took over local police stations and gave the orders. The local police hated it when the Special Branch stepped in and they had to play a subordinate role. When the commandant of the police station came in the next morning, I'd been there for several hours. He walked in with a stick under his arm like a big shot and said in Afrikaans, 'And why haven't I been told about this?' His men just said, 'Security.' He had no say in the matter.

Almost immediately I was pushed into a special room, a little reception area. The eight to ten men who had been at the house surrounded me. A rolled-up document lay on a table in front of me.

The men started shouting in my ears: 'You! You did this! You and Alex work together! We're trying to do something good for the country and you're working against us!' They were screaming and shouting right next to me.

'Shut up,' I said. 'I don't know what the hell you are saying. I can't hear. I can't talk to you. You are confusing me. I don't know what you want from me. I don't know what's going on.'

They were trying to get me to talk even before they locked me up. From the moment I walked in they wanted me to give information about my friends. They wanted me to say, 'Alex did it.'

Then the man who was in charge of the interrogation sent the others away. I was more fed up than scared. I now knew who I was dealing with.

He gave me the rolled-up paper, like a scroll. 'You delivered this document,' he said. 'Alex wrote this document, and you delivered it to various people.'

It wasn't in fact true.

'I've never seen this thing. I never delivered any documents at all.'

'How do you know? You haven't even read it,' he said. 'Open it up and read it.'

I'd been in the Movement long enough to know that he wanted me to touch the document so my fingerprints would be on it and then he could say, 'You did deliver it.'

'I've never handled anything like that,' I said. 'I'm not touching it. I don't even want to see what's in it.'

This man then called in one of the others. 'Sluit haar op! Neentig dae.' (Lock her up! Ninety days.) That was the first I knew I was to be detained for ninety days of solitary confinement. It was at this time in 1963 that ninety-day detention without trial was established, and I was among the first lot taken in.* I felt numbed, totally numbed.

They took me to my cell and left me to sweat it out. The cell was a large, clean room. After a few hours they brought in a young coloured woman who had been arrested for putting on her white madam's dress to go to a party. The madam reported her. Because I was supposed to be

---

* The 'Ninety-Day Detention Law' passed in May 1963 allowed for any person suspected of a political crime to be held for up to 90 days without access to a lawyer. The law was replaced in 1965 by one providing for 180-day detention and later by the Terrorism Act of 1967, which allowed for indefinite detention in solitary confinement.

in solitary confinement they had to pitch me out. I went from a good cell to a horrible one. By this time it was night.

My new cell was about eight by ten feet. Some cells were even smaller. I later found out that some of the men who were arrested couldn't even stretch out. I could at least walk around.

The ceiling was high with a window near the top. The cell was painted black three-quarters of the way up with the top quarter a dark grey. In the middle of the ceiling was the light, heavily meshed and so covered with dust that even in the middle of the day it cast a dull light. The cell was dark and bitterly cold.

The only thing to sit on was a coir mat, hard and scratchy, made from the hair of a coconut. My 'bed' was three stinking blankets placed on the mat, not even the full length of my body. The blankets were urine- and semen-stained, hard and smelly and infested with bedbugs. The bugs were tortoise-shaped – a little head at the top, little feet, and a big round blob at the back like a small tick, but brown in colour. And the stench! When I nursed some of my poorest patients I came home reeking of this smell of bedbugs.

There were so many bedbugs in the cell that they got between my fingers. I squeezed my hand to crush them. They also crawled up my legs, getting into every crevice of my body. When I sent my pyjamas home they were so filled with blood spots from the crushed bugs that my mother didn't know what was happening to me.

Worse yet, there were thousands of insects attacking me and entering every orifice of my face. God knows what they were! It was like a plague getting into my ears, nose and mouth. I'd cover my nose and they'd be in my ears. I'd cover my ears and they'd be in my eyes. I'd close my eyes and they'd go into my mouth. I couldn't open my mouth – I was afraid to breathe.

I went into total hysterics. I hammered the door so hard that I injured the little bone on my wrist. By then the police had left. They must have known what I was up against. Eventually I just settled down with all this muck around me. I then discovered the stench was also due to stagnant urine in the toilet, perhaps from people detained there overnight. The toilet was just a bowl, the origin of that cloud of mosquito-like insects.

I couldn't sleep that night because it was October and quite chilly. The cold night air blew in through the gap below the door. I was still in my nurse's uniform. I sat and froze in the muck around me. Then I lay down on the bare cement because the bugs had infested the coir mat. It was all I could do to keep warm. I didn't know where Alex was taken. I was kept awake by a nearby church clock that chimed every quarter-hour. It was terrible.

The next morning a policeman with a stick came into the cell, I suppose to see if I was still alive. People did try to commit suicide. He wasn't a Special Branch man but the superintendent-in-charge of the police station. I complained to him. 'This blanket is stinking. The place is dirty,' I said. 'I came here as a healthy woman. And if I get typhoid fever from this prison I'm suing you and the Minister of Justice for everything the country's got. My lawyer will hear about it.'

'Bring haar uit,' he said. (Bring her out.) Then he told the cleaner to clean the cell.

○

Whenever I was under tremendous stress I menstruated heavily, uncontrollably, even if I'd just had a cycle. I called it the Curse. And of course that's exactly what happened in detention. I bled uncontrollably and had nothing to protect myself. They'd torn up all my pads at home while they were looking for documents. So there I was in this bloody mess. I took off my shirt to clean myself. What else could I do?

I needed a wash and asked for a bucket of water. They wouldn't give it to me. I went to the wardress who was sitting at the door, stuck to her chair.

'I need help – certain help.'

'I can't help you,' she said. 'I'm not supposed to help you. There's nothing I can do about it.'

The next day the cleaner, a coloured man named Masonke, said to me, 'Missis, I am a married man, and I quite often have to go and buy these things for my wife. I will go and buy them for you.'

I said to him, 'You are a better man than my husband, because I would never ask him to buy these things. It's a very personal thing. But thank you very much. I appreciate it.'

Usually when you are detained they take everything from you, including your money. And yet they left my money – I had a rand or two in my uniform pocket. Why did they allow me to keep that? I think it was because they knew I would need the money to buy pads. The Special Branch wanted to humiliate and degrade me. The idea was to kill me by robbing me of every bit of dignity in my system.

But I maintained my dignity. That day Mr Masonke brought the pads, with the change. I accepted his generosity and washed myself. Then he had to buy another packet the next day because he could only bring one at a time. One packet was really not enough. The wardress sitting there said to him in Afrikaans, 'You don't bring her more. Only one packet.' It was part of the meanness of the whole situation.

Mr Masonke helped me throughout my detention. He couldn't speak to me every day, but only as opportunity arose, because the wardress was sitting there. While sweeping the floor or picking up the blankets he'd whisper something. Once he said to me in Afrikaans, 'Missis, your husband is also kept here. I can't say much, but your husband is here.' This confirmed what I already suspected. Alex had a distinctive cough from smoking, and when I heard his cough inside the prison I realised he wasn't far away.

○

I was told two days beforehand that I would be getting a visitor. I thought, 'Oh, they're bringing Eugene and Barto to see me. Or maybe they're bringing Alex. Or maybe my mother's coming.' I built up all this excitement for a visit. And then, unexpectedly, the visitors arrived: two big, burly Special Branch men whose job was to intimidate me.

I heard the keys rattling across the quad and quickly jumped to my feet. I didn't want these strange men looking down at me lying on the floor mat.

'Slaap jy nooit?' (Don't you ever sleep?) they asked, because I was on my feet.

'Nee, ek slaap nie.' (No, I don't sleep.)

One of them said: 'Mrs. La Guma [believe it or not, they called me Mrs La Guma], we've come to tell you that your son Eugene is very ill. He's got a chest infection. He's dying. If you answer our questions to our satisfaction, we'll allow you to go see him.'

The shock of what they said was almost too much. I was afraid I would collapse. 'I'm weak,' I thought. 'I'm going to fall. I mustn't give in.' Any sign of weakness and they could think they had me. I pushed myself hard up against the wall so I wouldn't collapse and dug my fingernails into the palm of my hand to cause pain. 'Feel the pain,' I told myself. 'Don't give in!'

I had to think quickly. They had done their homework. They knew about me and my menses and now they also knew Eugene had a chest problem. I hated to think that he was suffering. But then I thought, 'What if Eugene's illness wasn't true?' We had been informed by previous detainees that this kind of story had been put to them, only for them to find out that it wasn't true. These men knew the news would affect me badly. It was a ploy to get me to talk and implicate all my friends and comrades, or as many of them as possible. And then when they got what they wanted, I might find out that my child was all right.

I also thought, 'What do they mean that I must answer their questions to their satisfaction?' They wanted me to talk: 'What about your friends? What about your so-called comrades? You must have other comrades. You must know other people.' Even if I gave all my friends away, wouldn't these men just say, 'It's not to our satisfaction. You didn't give enough'? The answers would never be to their satisfaction, so they would keep on at you until you'd spilled the beans, and all for nothing.

If I betrayed any comrades in my cell, the Special Branch would hunt them down, find that lot and then the next lot and eventually bring the whole lot in. That would cripple us. Ninety-nine per cent of those who were killed lost their lives because somebody had spoken. Those I betrayed might not live. And I would not be able to live after that. I wouldn't be able to face my friends. That's when the words hit me: 'Don't betray! Tell them nothing! The answer is: No. No. No. No.'

It was a terrible decision to have to make. But I said to them: 'If my son is as ill as you say he is, then whoever has Eugene will do what I would do, and get him to a doctor. And if he needs further treatment, then you will let him go to your hospital, because you control the hospital and you control the whole bloody country.' I remember those words clearly. They could have refused to let him go to hospital, as mean as they were. They were fascists, the Nazis of South Africa.

They started calling me the dirtiest of communists. 'You are a dirty, filthy communist! It's only a dirty, filthy communist who would do what you are doing – let your child die and not even be there. What kind of mother are you?'

Then I thought, 'What if what they said about Eugene was true? What mother would allow this to happen to her child? A mother wouldn't. But I had something bigger to think about. I had all the other children to think about. I had the country to think about. No, I wouldn't give them what they wanted to know.'

'I don't know any others,' I told them. 'I don't know.'

They knew I was lying, but I wasn't about to give them what they wanted to hear, even if it meant I was taking a chance. I really wasn't sure *who* had charge of Eugene. Nevertheless, I had the feeling that my mother would never let me down. So I took the risk. Playing with my child's life was one of the biggest risks I ever had to take. It was terrible. I walked around my cell and wondered, 'What if he dies?' Only much later did I learn that Eugene wasn't ill.

And so I defied the Special Branch openly. To stand up against them was something in itself. But I was already in a mess. They couldn't do anything further to me. Solitary confinement was the worst I could get. They couldn't throw me into a deeper prison.

This was the end of my interrogation. They did not come back again. They let me sit and think about it, hoping that I wouldn't be able to take it any longer and would call them in to announce, 'Tell the Special Branch I've got something to say.' But I never did. Alex said later that I did the right thing. You don't betray your friends. You *never* betray.

Chapter 15

'Mommy, so you didn't run away from us?'

A dark cell drives you crazy. I tried to keep my brain going by doing little mental exercises: remembering a date, counting steps from one end of the cell to the other and then obliquely across. By the seventh day I felt I was going crazy. This hit me hard. Stupid ideas went through my mind. I didn't know what to think, what to do. I felt that if there was any way that I could get rid of myself, then I would. One is human and it becomes impossible to cope with solitary confinement. The idea of suicide seems real. I would have contemplated suicide more seriously if I had had the means to carry it out. But they take everything away just in case you want to try. They take away your belt. You've got no knife. You can't get rid of yourself.

After this moment passed, I just carried on. I had to simply stay there and wait until they released me. I thought I'd sing or try to keep myself busy in some other way, maybe walk up and down. I thought of my children. I missed my boys terribly, not knowing where they were or who was looking after them. And yet I couldn't cry. Even when I was released and saw Eugene and Barto, I thought I'd cry. But a knot came into my throat and I didn't. Even when Alex died years later, I couldn't cry. I had become hard fighting the whole apartheid system. We learned to be strong and not give in emotionally in difficult circumstances, because that was seen as a sign of weakness. The hardness stays with you, even when the circumstances are no longer there.

○

I knew I mustn't collapse, because the moment I did they'd find out and try to get me to talk. So I sang. I sang the songs and ballads that Alex and I used to sing. I'm fond of opera, so I imagined I was Mimi singing her arias in *La Bohème*. I sang American freedom songs like 'If I Had a Hammer'and 'We Shall Overcome' and of course, like any good Communist, 'The Internationale'. Funnily enough, when I sang 'The Internationale' one of the policemen came and hammered on my door saying, 'You're singing too beautifully. The police are supposed to be at their desks doing their work and they're all in the centre of the station listening to you singing.' They didn't even know what the song meant and would have been surprised to find out. Alex later said that when he heard someone sing 'The Internationale' he knew it could only be me. Likewise I knew Alex was there when I recognised his voice singing ballads we enjoyed at home.

Singing was an important part of the Struggle. In 1964 when Vuyisile Mini was led to the gallows he went singing freedom songs. He didn't do anything wrong; he fought apartheid. And yet he went to the gallows singing. That has stayed with me all these years.[*]

○

While in prison everything I wore went home to be washed by my mother. But before my sister-in-law Joan came to collect my clothes, I had in fact already washed them. I couldn't bear to think of Joan walking through the streets with my dirty underwear or going into the train with my dirty knickers. So with the half-bucket of cold water I was given each day, I first washed myself and then my clothes.

'Do you bath every day?' the wardress once asked.

'I bath once a day and wash three times,' I said. 'I am a nurse. And when I go to my next patient, I wash if there's a chance. So I wash very often.'

'Oh but that's too much,' she said. That shows the level of hygiene she had.

---

[*] Walter Sisulu recalled that Vuyisile Mini, a trade unionist from Port Elizabeth, entertained his fellow accused during the Treason Trial, leading them in song with his wonderful bass voice.

Every day when I did my kicking and jumping exercises in the courtyard, the wardress just sat there like a little chicken. I said to her, 'You are sitting here hooked to that chair. You are more imprisoned than I am. I am going home after this, but you are here permanently.'

'Yes,' she said in her thick Afrikaans accent. 'But it is my job.'

'It's a pretty lousy job, too,' I said.

Throughout my detention I never saw a bird, a tree or anything alive and moving except this half-dead woman sitting in her chair. She lived in an apartment upstairs with her husband, who was also a warder. She admired my lovely pyjamas because I don't think she had many nice clothes. When she took my clothes to hang on her line, it wasn't so much to help me as to try to impress her friends by pretending they were hers. A day or two later she came and told me that her husband had said she was not allowed to hang them out any more.

I didn't actually earn enough to buy fancy clothes and underwear. The good clothes I had were given to me by my friend Nancy Dick. She was the kind of person whose way of assisting others was to adopt them. Nancy would buy clothes or shoes for someone or pay for their schooling. She came from a wealthy family and had wealthy friends, the kind who wore a beautiful dress once or twice, then stopped wearing it because they were wealthy enough to buy another. Nancy had a friend the same size as I was, so she gave me this woman's clothes. Some of my friends said it was worth having a husband in politics, because I dressed beautifully. What they didn't know was that I hadn't paid a penny for my clothes. I couldn't – I had no money.

When Joan brought my clothes back, they were checked by the police, who opened every item and turned each pocket inside out to see that I wasn't receiving contraband. Though we weren't allowed reading material, my mother was able to line my suitcase with newspapers. After they caught me reading the newspaper they made sure nothing like that came in again.

○

I'd been detained several weeks when two Special Branch men came into the cell.

'Blanche, we've come to tell you that we're letting you go today,' one of them said in English. 'You're going home.'

I sat back and said nothing. I knew they had told others they could go home, only to meet them outside the prison gate and rearrest them. That's what they did to Ruth First and to Hennie Ferris, a CPC member from Worcester.* It was all part of the psychological torture. I was afraid they'd do this to me too.

'You can take your things and go,' they repeated.

I just sat there on a bundle of dirty prison blankets.

'What proof do I have that you're not going to rearrest me outside? You've done it to so many others. You might as well just leave me here.'

'No, Blanche,' they said. 'We won't rearrest you. We've been told you can leave.'

The Special Branch must have realised they were not going to get anything out of me. But that created a problem for me. The full term of solitary confinement was ninety days. Some detainees stayed that long and some were rearrested and stayed even longer. Ruth First was in for 117 days. But I had been in for only a few weeks. I was in a quandary. What might my friends think if I was released early? Had I spoken? Had I given anybody away? Had I betrayed? By letting me go, the Special Branch was giving my comrades the impression I had shopped them. I knew I hadn't betrayed anybody, but what would people think?

○

When I left Maitland Prison I was confused and disoriented. I'd been in a half-dark room for several weeks, and now I came out into the light. I didn't know which way to go and took the wrong turn, left towards Cape Town when I should have gone right towards Athlone. After a while I realised my mistake and returned to the police station, of all places, to get directions home. Eventually I found the railway station, bought a ticket, and went home.

While on the train I looked at myself and thought, 'Oh no.' I was still

---

* Hennie Ferris was a coloured CPC and ANC activist imprisoned with Mandela, Sisulu, Ahmed Kathrada, and others on Robben Island. Ferris's funeral in 1981 is cited as a key moment when the banned ANC emerged publicly with its flag defiantly hoisted by mourners.

in my prison overalls, not in the nice dress my mother had sent me to wear on my release. She always insisted that we look respectably dressed in the street. As she couldn't imagine me walking through the streets in my prison overalls, she sent the dress through Joan, and I put it neatly folded into my case ready to take out. But when they told me I could go, I was so eager to get out that I forgot about the dress. So there I was on the train in my prison overalls. I certainly did not want to be seen in that way.

When I arrived at our house in Garlandale, no one was home, so I went next door to get the key from Alex's mother and sister, who greeted me with hugs and tears.

'Where are the children?' I asked.

'The children are with your mother.' That was a tremendous relief. I knew my mother would not neglect them – spoil them maybe, but not neglect them. I then went back to our house and had a long, lovely bath, washed my hair and got ready for my father, who came down on his bicycle to take me to their house in Gleemoor to see Eugene and Barto. My mother was thrilled to see me. But when I went to the boys to give them a big hug, to my great surprise they shied away from me. It was such a shock. In the days that followed, the boys completely ostracised me. They didn't talk with me or even answer me. They wouldn't have anything to do with me. They just gave me dirty looks. I didn't know why the children were reacting this way. They wouldn't say why, either. No one knew what the problem was, not even my mother, who had taken care of them the whole time.

A couple of weeks later we were invited to lunch at the home of my good friend Rita Tabakin. It was the first time I had the chance to tell Rita and her husband Morris about solitary confinement. Barto and Eugene sat at the table with us. When I told the Tabakins how the arrest took place, four-year-old Barto said: 'Mommy, so you didn't run away from us?'

'No, darling. I didn't run away from you.'

'Your Mommy was detained,' my friends said.

'Mr Genis and Mr Van Wyk said that you had run away,' Barto went on. He didn't say anything further but took hold of me and gave me a big hug and warm kiss, as did Eugene. Only then did they believe that I had not deserted them but was detained in prison.

The boys had originally accepted that I had been arrested. In fact, Eugene tearfully told Mrs Dixon that his parents had gone to prison to make life better for Barto and him and other children, echoing what I told him whenever Alex was arrested. But Genis and Van Wyk met Eugene one day after school and told him I had run away. In his young mind this made a kind of sense. Eugene knew that Mommy had never been arrested, so why did everybody now say I had been arrested? No, that couldn't be, he thought; Daddy was the one who was always arrested; Mommy was always there. Now suddenly Mommy was gone. So the lies from Genis and Van Wyk worked.

There was one other unfortunate consequence of my detention. After my return home Barto started behaving like a baby. Previously he used to play with the neighbours' children, go to nursery school, and even sleep over at a friend's house. But now he was insecure and leaned even more heavily on Eugene, who was quite patient and tender towards him. Even when I told Barto that I hadn't run away, he seemed to be afraid that I would. He wanted to be by my side all the time, following me around and even grabbing hold of me when I moved. He also started bedwetting. I had been worried that my detention would have a bad effect on the boys, but I had no idea it would hurt either of them in this way or to this extent.

○

While in detention I lost my midwifery practice. Nobody knew when I was going to be released and patients couldn't wait for me to be set free. When they realised I was home, they came to book me, some for the first time. Many had other nurses, and it was the practice among nurse-midwives not to take another nurse's patients. When new patients came to me I said, 'Won't you go back to your nurse, please, because she must have treated you well.'

Most of them replied, 'Nurse, my husband says I must book you because you are fighting and doing the job we are afraid to do. You even go to jail for us. We must support you, and this is one way to do that. I'm going to have a baby. I'll have to pay for this baby, and I prefer to book you as my nurse.' It was heart-rending. I almost wept when I heard this because I knew then that we had the support of the community.

○

Alex was in prison and I didn't have any money. I had *nothing*, absolutely nothing. Not a crumb of bread. The boys were used to eating around five o'clock when I'd call them inside. One day it was already six o'clock and I had nothing in the house to eat.

Eugene ran past the house to his hiding place. 'Mommy, not five o'clock yet?' he said. He was hungry, but he was too diplomatic to tell me directly.

'No darling, it's not five o'clock yet,' I lied. 'In a short while Mommy's going to buy something to eat.'

I thought I would borrow some money from my mother. But just as I was about to set out a patient came up and said, 'Nurse, I went to work this morning and my daughter complained of tummy ache, so I put some leaves on her tummy. I've come home now, and the baby's born. Can you please come and cut the cord and see to her? Nurse, I've only got two pounds.'

I scolded her. 'You left your daughter on her own in this difficult time. I'll come,' I said. 'You've got two pounds. Take one pound and buy something for your family. I'll take the other pound.' When I finished attending to the girl and her baby, I took the pound to the shop and bought something to eat that night and for breakfast the next morning.

We weren't always so fortunate or self-sufficient. During these tough times when we had little money I couldn't have made it without the help of friends. Even though I had left St Monica's five or six years earlier, Matron Hoey-Jones and Dr Barrow, the superintendent, both fine women strongly opposed to apartheid, as well as Sisters Tilbrook and Legg, always considered me part of the hospital. Without my even asking they brought parcels of tea, coffee, sugar, fruit, and some sweets for the boys. They knew I was fighting apartheid and they were eager to help one of the St Monica's people going through a difficult time. It was really very warming.

Later, when I was banned, the nursing sisters came to visit me. They knew I could only speak with one person at a time, so Matron would come into the house while Sisters Tilbrook and Legg sat outside in the car. Then they'd rotate and take turns coming in and saying hello.

○

When I returned from detention I had fallen behind in my accounts. While my mother was taking care of the boys, she and my father were pensioners and had a hard time making ends meet. My lawyer Himie Bernadt advised her to get assistance from the Board of Aid. At first the Board refused to help, saying they did not assist families of political prisoners. But after my mother reported the matter to Himie, he intervened and only then did she receive a food parcel and a small amount of money for milk and meat.

When I was released this bit of assistance was stopped. But then the Black Sash came to my rescue. The Black Sash Advice Office played a big role in the struggle, advising women about the complicated requirements of the pass system, which the Black Sash opposed, and giving out food parcels to women whose husbands were detained.

The bureau was headed by Mrs Mary Stoy, an active member. I had earlier said to Mrs Stoy, 'I don't need help while I am working. I will only come when I need your help.' Even though I was earning little, I was at least working. One way or another I was able to meet my financial liabilities. As other women whose husbands were detained were not working, I felt that any financial assistance should go to them.

After my detention, though, I was badly in need of help. I'd fallen behind in my rent and rates, and especially the electricity bill, which was quite high. I took my rent bill and my electricity bill of £9 to the Advice Office, which was not far from my house, in Klipfontein Road in Athlone. As Mrs Stoy was out for the moment, a colleague on duty went through all the drawers and boxes in the office but could not find any record of my file. I had to wait for Mrs Stoy to arrive so she could identify me. When she walked in she said, 'Oh Mrs La Guma, I'm so glad to see you're out.' Her colleague told her he couldn't find my file. Mrs Stoy said, 'She doesn't have a file. Mrs La Guma said she would only come when she needs us, and she definitely needs us now.' The Advice Office then promptly settled my bills.

◯

Alex stayed in detention for the full ninety days. When he came out in early 1964 he went back into house arrest. From 1962 until we left the country in 1966, each time he was detained he was released back into house arrest. He went from prison on the outside to prison inside his home.

Though Alex was never physically tortured, he was mentally tortured – hour after hour of questioning, and always threats. Alex and I didn't speak to each other about our interrogation because we were still working clandestinely in different cells. Talking might have given away our association with particular comrades and made us vulnerable in further detentions. I did, though, tell Alex how the Special Branch had threatened me with Eugene's illness.

Incredibly, the Special Branch returned our books to my mother while we were still in prison, even the works of Marx and Lenin. I'm sure they didn't read them. If they did, how much could they have understood?

Chapter 16

'We will stay, and Eugene will take his chances with the rest'

Apartheid took its toll not only on us but on our children as well. It required that they grow up much more quickly than they would ordinarily have done.

When Eugene was just five, I was working while Alex was away or in prison. With no adults at home, I needed Eugene to stay in the house near the telephone so that when it rang he could, in his way, take messages, particularly from patients who needed my care. He hadn't yet learned how to write, so he invented his own written script. He would write down marks or symbols he could remember and later relay their meaning to me. When I came home he could tell me very clearly: 'Mommy, Mrs Williams is expecting a baby. You must go to her quickly. Mrs Abrahams – she's only wanting you to come and visit her. And Mrs So-and-so wants you to come and examine her.' Fortunately, I could go through the list of patients' names in my register and find out exactly who had phoned and what was going on. He was really good – he never made one mistake. It was amazing that I could rely on a five- or six-year-old boy, but it was so unfair, too. He carried an enormous amount of responsibility at an early age and couldn't play freely outside like the other children. It was rather cruel of me to expect this of him, but what else could I do?

Eugene took on many important responsibilities at an early age. When Alex was detained I told him, 'Each time Daddy goes, then you are the Daddy and Barto is the big brother.' I gave Eugene little tasks to do. He made sure the door was locked at night and the windows were closed. He helped around the house and did small errands like buying bread, milk, and vegetables, which also meant he had to learn how to handle money. Barto's job was to see that the papers were picked up in the yard, the place wasn't dirty, and the bins were clean. The boys did their chores well.

Because Barto was younger and didn't have the responsibility that Eugene had, he took life easier. He was happy-go-lucky. Once as I walked home, I found Barto happily sitting up on a horse-drawn refuse cart. 'The Uncle said I could ride the horses,' he said. (Everybody was 'uncle' to him.) The man had given Barto the reins and he was feeling just on top of the world.

◯

When I returned from detention and Alex was still in prison, I started receiving calls from the security police threatening to kidnap the children. 'We can even dress up like your father,' I remember them saying. At the time my father had been fetching the boys from school, one at a time, on the back of his bicycle. He'd been doing this since before my detention, because when I went out on a case at three or four in the morning, I didn't know if I'd be back in time to take the boys to school. My father was happy to help us and the boys enjoyed the ride.

I was shocked when the Special Branch threatened to kidnap my children by disguising one of their number as my father. Though it was just a bluff and I don't think the boys would have been fooled by the disguise, it worried me all the same. Sometimes I felt I just couldn't cope. Among all the calls I received from the Special Branch, this one was especially horrible.

I left a note with Barto's teacher at nursery school telling her not to give him to anybody until I came. I also told Barto, 'Don't go with anyone but me.' By this time I had been banned and couldn't enter the school grounds, according to the banning order. Every day I stood outside waiting for somebody to pass by. I'd give him or her a penny and say, 'Please go inside and tell the teacher that Barto's mother is here.'

Once when I got to Barto's school late, he was the only one there with his teacher, Miss Manning. When he came out he said, 'You know, Mommy, I thought you runned away from me.'

'Mommy was on a case,' I said. 'I want to be the one to fetch you. I don't want to give you to anybody else. I'm getting jealous now because Grandpa's been coming to fetch you.' I didn't tell him about the kidnapping threat. He was only a nursery school boy.

○

When Eugene and Barto were quite young, Genis and Van Wyk started harassing the boys. They wanted to find out from them who was visiting their Daddy, because under house arrest Alex was not allowed visitors except for a lawyer and doctor who were not banned. Because I was banned, even I had to receive the magistrate's permission to live with Alex, though we were married and had two children.

Genis and Van Wyk waited for the boys after school or caught them on the road or while playing in the street. They harassed them and asked them questions, and they weren't soft about it, either. Their aim was to frighten and bully them so that out of fear the boys would say, 'Yes, So-and-so did see my Daddy.' Being the older of the two, Eugene had to carry the brunt of it all. Poor Eugene: he was trapped. But he was a strong character and just said, 'No, nobody saw my Daddy.' When the boys were together and the men asked Barto about Alex, he'd let Eugene answer because Eugene could tell a lie better than he could. Barto was small and was probably afraid of saying the wrong thing.

When Eugene was six years old and waiting to be fetched from primary school, Genis and Van Wyk really worked him over. Eugene would run back and forth between the two school gates trying to get away from them. They'd catch him and push him around, really just to try to drive fear into him. Or they'd offer him a sweet and when he put his hand out they'd take the sweet away. He'd come home crying, telling us what they had done to him.

Once when Eugene and Barto were playing in the street they saw the car approaching that Genis and Van Wyk drove. The children knew the different cars of the Special Branch – the blue sedans and the little white Volkswagens. When they saw the car stop, they ran away in different directions. Eugene hid under a neighbour's car and waited until Genis and Van Wyk had finished searching the house.

After they left, we couldn't find him. He'd just vanished. It was getting dark and I was growing more afraid. I stood at the gate and began calling for him.

 After a while I heard a faint, small voice: 'Mommy, here I am.'

He came crawling out from under the neighbour's car.

'I'm here, Mommy. Have they gone?'

Only later did I realise that my neighbour might have got into the car without seeing Eugene and driven off.

○

No matter what they did to Eugene, he would never tell the police who was visiting his Daddy. Once Alex's friend Achmat Osman came to visit. Ozzie, as we knew him, had been subpoenaed to give evidence against a banned person who had attended a meeting in violation of his banning order. Ozzie refused to give evidence and now his own case was pending at the magistrate's court.

While he was visiting Alex, Eugene saw Genis and Van Wyk arrive and ran to tell us. He knew his Daddy shouldn't be sitting in the room with Uncle Ozzie. As he approached the outside gate he shouted, 'Daddy, Mr Genis and Mr Van Wyk are here!' Alex then went to a back room while Ozzie and I stood in the kitchen.

Genis and Van Wyk caught Eugene in front of the kitchen door and started pushing and pulling him around. They could see Ozzie and me in the kitchen.

'No, nobody saw my Daddy,' Eugene said. 'Uncle Ozzie didn't speak with my Daddy. My Daddy's working in a room. Only my Mommy spoke with Uncle Ozzie.'

That's when they smacked him. 'You're lying. You warned them we were coming.'

Alex came out when he heard this.

'Stop beating my children!' he said. 'Look what you're doing!'

'Just shut up or we'll take all of you and lock you up!' they threatened. They could have done it, too, even if only to put Alex in prison for a night to frighten him.

Barto was standing next to me. He grabbed one of the men's legs. 'Don't hit my brother! Leave my brother alone!'

They took hold of Barto and pushed him. After he'd fallen I picked him up. It was horrible to see my children treated like this. I wanted to fly in a rage at these men. But one of them had a gun and was waving it around. The gun was meant for Eugene, who was only six years old. What could we do?

Genis and Van Wyk searched the house and of course they couldn't find anything. Then they left.

I said to Alex, 'You know, I think the time has really come for us to go. Look what's happening to these children. Look what's happening to Eugene. They're ruining him.'

Alex looked right at me.

'You're thinking only of Eugene,' he said. 'What about the other children? Have you thought of Sarah's children? Have you thought of Zollie's children? Ruth's? Nelson's? Walter's?* They are all going through the same thing.'

Then he said what my heart did not want to hear. 'We will stay,' Alex said, 'and Eugene will take his chances with the rest.'

I went to the toilet and wept bitterly. I thought, 'What is going to happen?' But I knew Alex was correct. It wasn't only about our children. It was about other people's children as well. It was then that I resolved to toughen up Eugene. He had to stand and grow up very fast, rather cruelly at an early age. At the time I didn't know when or even if we were going to leave the country. What if we were to stay? So I had to toughen both of them up for what was going to come. I knew that if they grew up in South Africa they would be part of the Struggle, and God knows what might happen.

I made it clear to the boys that they had to grow up faster than other children. They couldn't cry. They had to stand up for themselves. There was no other way. Though you babied them and loved them no less than any other parent would, you had a larger commitment as well. The struggle was not only about you and your children.

---

* Sarah Carneson, Zollie Malindi, Ruth First, Nelson Mandela and Walter Sisulu.

When Lucilla Blankenberg, who made a documentary film of my life, asked Eugene, 'What did you think of your mother?' he replied, 'Bitch.' I don't blame him. I wasn't hurt by that. I *was* a bitch, after all. But I couldn't tell him when he was a boy, 'I'm raising you one day to fight Genis and Van Wyk.' I just kept quiet and in my own way made them stronger without their realising it.

Later on in the day when Eugene was beaten by Genis and Van Wyk, he actually apologised to me. 'Mommy, I know you don't want me to lie. I'd tell the truth, but I was afraid my Daddy would go to prison again.' He knew that when Genis and Van Wyk came to the house it could mean imprisonment for Alex, whom he was trying to protect. So he told a lie and then apologised for telling it, even though at the time they manhandled him in front of us.

I told him, 'You did the right thing, Eugene. You thought very well. Mommy can't teach you when you must tell the truth. That is something you have to learn on your own.'

○

On one occasion while out shopping with Eugene, I bought him an ice cream. He went over to a table to sit and join a little white boy who was also enjoying an ice cream. When he was told by the white shop supervisor that he was not allowed to sit there, I remarked for all to hear – and the shop was full of people – that we were allowed to spend our money but not allowed to sit at the table to eat.

I turned to Eugene. 'That is why your Daddy is in prison, so that you too can sit at the table and eat your ice cream, not only little white boys. This is what apartheid does and your Daddy is fighting against apartheid.'

Eugene was as hurt as I was, but he learned in a practical manner what apartheid meant. I felt much better that my audience in the shop heard what I had to say. Hopefully some of the people learned something, not only for Eugene's good or mine, but for their own too.

◯

When Alex was arrested for the last time in 1966, he was taken away in the morning just as Eugene and Barto were getting ready for school. We stood at the gate waving goodbye to him. Suddenly, Eugene collapsed and fell to the ground. I quickly pulled him up and told him he must be strong, as his Daddy was trying to make a better life for him and all children. Perhaps that seems harsh but I didn't know what else to say. It was ridiculous to expect him to understand what was happening, although he tried hard to understand. It was difficult for both of us. I told him to go to school, work hard, and do his best that day to get all his sums correct so that when his Daddy came home he could show him how hard he had worked and how he appreciated what his Daddy was doing for him.

When I took him to school I spoke with his teacher and told her what had happened that morning. I asked her to treat Eugene in the usual way and not fuss too much around him. I didn't want him to grow up feeling sorry for himself. But I said that if he showed signs of being different, then I knew she'd understand and would deal with the matter without treating him too harshly.

That afternoon when I fetched him he ran to me saying, 'Look, Mommy! I got a star for getting all my sums right. I'm going to show my Daddy.'

◯

Looking back at how I raised Eugene and Barto, I always wonder if I did the right thing. Raising children in the circumstances of my life was quite difficult. Did I make a success of it? I sometimes felt I was quite cruel. But I couldn't cope in any other way.

Barto put me straight one day. He was in his twenties living on his own and he had come back home. I was flitting around him all the time. 'Can I do this? What can I give you? Can I give you that? What about breakfast? Can I—'

I was trying too hard and he sensed it.

'Mom! I've been on my own for a long time, you know. I do all these things myself. I know what it is,' he went on. 'You're trying to make up because you think you neglected us when we were small. You didn't, Mom. You did the right thing. If you had raised us the way that you wanted to, we would have been two complete cabbages. We would not have been able to cope going abroad. Eugene went to Moscow – a different society, a different country and language – and he coped. I went to Germany, the GDR, and I met different people and learned a different language, and I coped. You didn't do wrong.'

It was a wonderfully comforting message from him.

○

I once asked Eugene, 'Do you feel hard done by because you carried a bigger burden than Barto?'

'No, I didn't find it a strain,' he said. 'You raised us to realise that we have to fight for our own freedom.'

I had in fact often said to them, 'Even *you* have to fight for your freedom. You also must be able to do things for yourself, and not only have Mommy and Daddy do things for you.'

○

As a boy Barto loved to climb the tree in our garden, though Alex was afraid he would fall. Alex had lived in the city all his life and was a typical city slicker. There was really no room to play in Cape Town, especially in District Six where he grew up. He never rode a bicycle; he never climbed a tree. So to make sure Barto didn't fall, Alex put sticks across the tree to make a ladder. Barto got rid of the sticks and flew up the tree like a monkey.

Once when he was up in the tree he looked down and said, 'I've found a *katokkie*!' *Katokkie* is Afrikaans for an acorn.

'My God,' Alex said. '*Katokkie*? It's a blinking bug they put up there!'

Barto thought he had found an acorn. But Alex immediately realised it was a recording device, a bug planted by the police. The Special Branch knew we would speak with others under the tree because we were aware the house was bugged.

Barto had the right idea, though. He thought it was an acorn so he pulled the device right off. And why not? He had found it, and it was his to keep.

○

My tears flow when I relive these stories about my sons. Neither Alex nor I could defend our children. The Special Branch could easily have taken Eugene or even the whole family to prison, if only for a few hours. If Alex or I had challenged Genis and Van Wyk, the effect on the boys, especially Eugene, would have been traumatic. These men were the meanest of people. I can never forget what they did.

Blanche with Barto and Eugene, 1965

Chapter 17

'What happened last night is exactly what the Special Branch wants'

My relationship with Alex worked well because it wasn't just a romance. We thought alike. We had the same attitudes about life, even about raising our children. Before we were married Alex had lots of other girlfriends, but I never got jealous. My attitude was, if he's chosen me as his girlfriend and is not able to endure a commitment, then I don't want him – I don't want any man like that.

When he was involved in the Treason Trial for three years, I was one of the few Cape Town wives who didn't go to Johannesburg. 'Don't you think he might be having an affair?' someone would ask.

'If he is, he always still comes back to me,' I said. 'And if he's so weak that another woman can just take him over, then I don't want him.' If a man can't overcome the temptation of another woman, what other temptations can he not overcome? I mean, that would be a burden to me. Better to be rid of him.

I made my attitude abundantly clear to him, even later when we lived in London and he became a high-profile international writer and political activist. There were a couple of girls who were keen on him that I knew about. But I never for one moment feared he would drop me for one of them.

He knew that he could also trust me. When I made that historic trip to Durban in 1961 as the only woman with three chaps in the car, he said, 'So, you're leaving me?'

'For a short while. I've been sent to do something important. I don't know what it is.'

'OK, then. I'll look after Eugene.'

He knew it was a matter of sheer trust. It goes with any marriage.

At one stage while we were living in London he told me that some of his friends were leaving their wives. Though ours was a stable relationship, even so, I thought, before I'm caught unawares I'd better make sure about Alex in case I need to start preparing for a life of my own.

I approached him and said, 'Look, I'm becoming quite nervous now. Our friends are leaving their wives and running away with other women. If you're having an affair, tell me. I don't care what happens. It will just be very hurtful. Just don't let it become a real stink. Be a man and make a clean break.'

'Good heavens!' he said. 'What is the purpose of this conversation? Are you mad?'

'You are internationally known,' I said. 'If it happens, come to me – as cruel and as hard as it may be – and say: "I've found another woman. The party's over." If we don't get on any longer, I'll accept that. It happens in many families. Just don't deceive me.'

I said all of this because I'd given up a lot for Alex. I had supported him throughout our life together. Our level of trust had to be one hundred per cent.

'I'd have to be crazy, Blanche, to go after every woman that comes along.'

'I'm just trying to make clear what my feelings are,' I said. 'This time I'm thinking of Blanche and of Blanche's future; I'm thinking of Eugene and Barto. I must prepare them —'

'Look,' he said. 'I can't fall in love with every beautiful woman I meet when I travel.'

'No, you can't,' I said, 'because I'm the most beautiful woman!'

○

Ours was a good marriage. It was a good partnership, and a good understanding, which is not the case in all marriages. Despite the difficulties, he understood me, and I understood him. But sometimes it was difficult. When he was under house arrest for five years and I was banned at the same time, the two of us together became too much for each other at times. We would drive each other round the bend. He was terribly tense at times, worried that his writing would be taken away in a police raid, as sometimes happened. I was in a daze from working night and day to keep the family together. The strain on both of us was hard, quite often leading to a clash. I'd go into a fit of anger from something small he'd done and leave the house in a rage. I'd slam the door shut and walk out, saying I was going to my mother or my friends. But when I reached the gate it would occur to me, 'So you can go, but he cannot. He's under house arrest. He's also angry, but he cannot leave.' Then I'd come back into the house and say, 'You want some tea?'

One Friday evening five of us were at home, including a teenager named Mary who helped with the boys. Alex had been under house arrest for four years and I think it finally got to him. He was walking around like a caged lion. He started throwing things, I think because of something I said. He threw a great big electric kettle that just missed me. Then he took a little stool in front of the dressing table and threw that. It caught my shoulder. It was the first time I thought he had gone berserk.

Alex was having a nervous breakdown – that's what I called it. He was going to attack someone and the nearest target was me. But he didn't do anything to Mary or the children. They witnessed it all. Eugene said later, 'My Daddy's very ill.'

I ran next door to his parents' house to seek refuge. They must have heard all the noise because when I knocked on the door, my sister-in-law Joan opened it part of the way but wouldn't let me in.

When I told her what had happened she said, 'You must be glad to be married to my brother. You must remember, he is a La Guma.'

'And a rubbish at that!' I said.

She shut the door in my face.

The La Gumas were highly thought of in the community, and now it seemed she was blaming me for the situation. I couldn't help the fact that he was under house arrest.

There I was standing outside, an exile from my own house. I didn't know what to do. I didn't want to go to my mother and get her involved.

I thought, 'No, this is my home and this is where I'm going to stay. Another thing: I must be there to protect the children.' So I went back in.

For the rest of the day we skirted each other, saying little. That night I went into our room and got into bed next to him. 'Alex,' I said, 'this is my bed. This is where I'm going to sleep, and this is where I'm going to stay.'

He didn't answer. He was terribly ashamed. I said nothing more because I thought, 'What's the point? I'll wait until morning.'

I didn't sleep much that night. The next morning I got up early, bathed the children and got them ready. Saturday was the day I fetched my mother with the car and we'd go shopping in Athlone. First, though, I visited some patients while my mother and the boys sat in the car. By the time I'd finished with my patients and walked back to the car, Eugene had told my mother the entire story as he understood it. She and Eugene were very close. When I got into the car she asked what had happened the previous night. I told her it seemed that Alex had lost his head.

'We'll go and do this shopping,' I said. 'But when we get home I'd prefer that you don't come in with me, because I'm really going to have go to town on him and make things abundantly clear. It's make-up-your-mind time now about the future.'

When we got home, Alex was in the yard fixing a fence. I went to him and said, 'What happened last night is exactly what the Special Branch wants. You are playing right into their hands. It's *not* going to happen again.'

I spoke firmly with him. I told him he would just have to pull up his socks and know that he couldn't perform like this because if he did I was going to leave him. I had to think of the children.

'You're under house arrest. You can't get out of that,' I said. 'But you will just have to bear with it. You went in for this political thing, they put you under house arrest, and this is the result. It's too much. It's too much for both of us. I can't walk out. But I'll have to do so if you don't behave yourself.'

Alex apologised profusely. He said he didn't know what had happened. He had just gone off, really lost it, not deliberately, but uncontrollably. I realised he was not to blame: he couldn't help it. His circumstances were to blame. He wasn't allowed to see anybody; he couldn't leave the house; and he couldn't write. He'd write something and then the Special Branch would raid the house and collect everything he'd written and take it away.

For the most part, Alex was remarkably calm during his house arrest. His outburst happened only once. It was terrible, but it never happened again.

◯

I value my time with Alex so very much. A friend who was breaking up with her husband asked, 'How do you and Alex manage?' I said to her, 'He is my lover, my mentor, my everything.'

There's a saying in communism: 'From each according to his ability, to each according to his needs.' That was a slogan we lived out in our marriage. I fully supported Alex financially. There was never much money, but there was always food. I was able to work and keep things going in the family. He couldn't do that under house arrest. He needed me.

On the other hand, I learned a lot from him. His political intellect was important for the Movement and for me. Sometimes I couldn't understand the heavier stuff. While we were in England there were times when I'd read the *World Marxist Review,* a monthly magazine published in Czechoslovakia, and not understand a thing.

'Alex, I don't understand this. Why can't they bring these things down to a level where one can understand?'

'No, no, no,' he'd say. 'You will have to raise your level to understand.'

That upset me! 'But I can't make sense of it,' I said. 'I can't even read it.'

Then he'd patiently explain things by coming down to my level.

But still it might come to nothing, and if I didn't understand, I couldn't sleep. I'd wake Alex in the middle of the night, asking him once again to explain. One more time he'd patiently explain Marxist theory. He was one in a million with his patience. He wouldn't complain but would explain things until I was happy. The moment I got it I'd say, 'OK, now I understand.' Then I'd fall back to sleep. Unfortunately, he was now awake and would have to read himself back to sleep.

Chapter 18

'Think of leaving. Decided'

In 1965 Alex was detained at the Woodstock police station under a new law extending solitary confinement to 180 days. I was banned and confined to the magisterial district of Wynberg. Since Woodstock was in the magisterial district of Cape Town, I needed permission from the magistrate to leave Wynberg to visit Alex once a month for thirty minutes, and even that required a good reason to see him in the view of the apartheid state. On one occasion Alex's mother was in hospital with a breast complaint, and I used it as an excuse for getting a visit to Alex, saying that his mother wanted to be reassured he was well. I was given permission, but not before the security police went to Groote Schuur Hospital to enquire whether my mother-in-law was in fact telling the truth.

Each visit with Alex was non-contact, with the police at every window and exit. No politics were to be spoken, only family matters. In the room where we met, the security police listened to every word we spoke. As soon as I said something about family or relatives that the police thought had crossed the line into politics, the visit was stopped even before the half-hour was up. The Special Branch even placed electronic equipment on the table where I sat so that they could pick up everything I said, despite the presence of policemen all around us.

○

Once my lawyer, Himie Bernadt, asked me to visit Alex to see if he might give evidence in a case involving his friend Fred Carneson. Fred had been charged with something – I'm not sure what – and Alex had been his accomplice. I think they were working in a cell together and that's why the two of them were arrested. The security police wanted Alex to give evidence against Fred, who was going to make certain statements about what he (Fred) had done. It wasn't a matter of Fred giving away names or saying anything about Alex. But Himie wanted Alex to give evidence against Fred, though he didn't think that what Alex might say would be harmful to Fred. It was a way of protecting Alex without getting Fred into any deeper trouble.

When I went to see Alex and told him what Himie suggested, his reaction nearly caused the breakup of our marriage. He was *furious*, absolutely furious.

'You come here and tell me to be a traitor? To betray Fred? What do you think Fred and Sarah are going to think of me?'

The police were sitting around, trying to listen in.

'What are my other comrades going to think of me?' He looked at me and said, 'This visit is over!'

'But you haven't asked —'

He just marched out.

I yelled after him: 'The children are fine.'

The little Alex could have said against Fred wouldn't have been much. But the point was that he'd been asked to give evidence against his comrade. You gave your life for your comrade, you didn't give evidence against him. Do it once and you became a roaming ambassador of betrayal: the Special Branch used you to go around the country and give evidence against everybody else. You'd rather die than to do that.

As it turned out, Fred made certain statements which in fact cleared Alex, who was then released after four or five months – short of the 180 days. Fred admitted to some of what he had done and got only five years instead of a heavier sentence. I say 'only' five because Sarah told me that when she went up to Fred after the sentencing he remarked, 'Only five years.' He knew that he could have got a much longer sentence.[*]

---

[*] Fred Carneson was one of the last remaining leaders of the white Congress of Democrats and part of the Communist Party underground in Cape Town until his trial in the mid-1960s. According to Albie Sachs's book *Stephanie on Trial*, Carneson admitted certain details at his trial in order to protect others from having to give evidence.

○

While Alex was still in confinement in 1966, Himie asked me to relay the message that the ANC had decided he should think of leaving the country when he was released. The ANC felt that Alex could no longer be effective in the Struggle as he was constantly under house arrest or in detention. He could make a bigger contribution overseas working freely at the international level.

I thought hard about how I would get the message to Alex. Eventually, I got an idea. I wrote a small note on firm paper: 'Think of leaving.' In bold type I wrote: '*Decided.*' I boiled a small potato and, when it was soft, I inserted the note and smoothed it over. I gave the potato a quick fry in a little cooking oil until it was crisp and brown and then placed the potato into a pie and covered it with pastry. Alex liked potatoes and I knew he'd suspect there was something in that small, lonely potato.

I thought Alex might not believe my message, if he received it at all. When Eugene was harassed by the security police and I told Alex we should leave the country, he rejected the idea. I thought Alex might respond in the same way when he was released. I even told my mother not to come home with me for our usual tea after shopping because I thought Alex and I would argue. But Alex believed what I had written.

'Since you placed the smallest potato you could find in the pie that you sent me,' he said, 'and since it is decided, we'll go.'

But first Alex wanted to confirm this message with the ANC; he didn't just take my word. It was only after I got confirmation from Zollie Malindi, ANC chairman in the Western Cape, did we start making efforts to leave the country.

Surprisingly in view of its eagerness to get rid of us, the regime made our leaving very difficult. Because I was banned, I had to apply for permission to leave the country. Alex had to apply for permission just to leave his house and then again to leave the country. After we received these permissions, we applied for passports. But instead of passports we were given exit permits, which meant we could not return to South Africa. In effect, we were deprived of our citizenship. When I asked

Genis whether my children might be allowed to return, he said to me: 'No La Guma will *ever* be allowed to return to South Africa while we are in power.'

When we applied for our visas, the consul-general of the United Kingdom came to our house. He explained that he had been sent by his government to interview us since the restrictions imposed on us meant we could not see him at the consulate in the city. He was a polite man. It was the first time, he said, that a consul-general had ever gone to the applicants' house for the interview.

The British must have done their research on us, judging by the questions he asked. He knew of our detentions and bannings and of Alex's political life since the Treason Trial. Then came the cardinal question: 'You were a member of the central committee of the South African Communist Party. If the Party became legal and you were again elected to that position today, would you accept it?'

'Yes,' Alex firmly replied.

'And you, Mrs La Guma, will you again join the Party?'

'Yes,' I said.

When he had gone, I said to Alex, 'There go our visas to the UK.' But about two months later we received word that we had been accepted and would be leaving on 21 September 1966.

When we told Eugene (then ten) and Barto (seven) that we were leaving, they weren't concerned about going away; they were just excited. 'Barto,' Eugene said, 'we're going up in a jet!'

In leaving the country, our final challenge was to get to the airport. When I tried to make arrangements for a taxi, I was shocked to find out the security police had warned the taxi drivers that if they took us to the airport they would lose their licences. Regrettably, they told me, they could not take us. Even in getting rid of us, the Special Branch wanted to make things as difficult as possible.

I called Dolly Wiid, a close friend who always supported me. I asked her to arrange taxis for us, even if that meant one from Cape Town for

Alex and another from Wynberg for me. I reckoned the security police couldn't get to every taxi.

'No, Blanche,' Dolly said, 'I will take you myself.'

'Dolly, do you realise what this means for your future? They're going to hound and harass you. Life will be impossible.'

'I am your *friend* and I will take you,' she said. And with that firm reply I accepted her offer.

We were given permission to leave on a specific day and told to report at the airport at three o'clock. When we left our house the Special Branch were waiting in several cars. Our neighbours, who always supported us, came out into the street to wave us goodbye, in tears and sad to see us go. As we drove to the airport in Dolly's car we saw a police car in front and two cars on each side. They were escorting us out of the country like celebrities.

At the airport ten Special Branch men stood waiting, making sure we didn't transgress any law. Barto said, 'See, there's Mr Van Wyk! There's Mr Genis!' The boys knew them both. These were the same men Eugene had yelled at during the State of Emergency in 1960 when they came with guns drawn against Alex.

When we had been through customs and immigration, there at the exit to the plane was a huge crowd of people. I said to Alex, 'Someone important must be leaving today.' Lo and behold, it was people coming to say goodbye to us – people who knew Alex from his political work in places like Paarl, Wellington, Stellenbosch and Robertson. They had come all that way to say goodbye, joining our friends from Cape Town. But Alex was not allowed to speak with anybody, and I was allowed to have only two people speaking with me. So my mother, my mother-in-law, and Eugene and Barto had to push the people away and tell them why they could not talk with us. They just had to stand aside and wave. Any gesture from Alex would have been interpreted by the Special Branch as a form of communication, so he stood facing the wall with his back to his well-wishers.

For the occasion I bought a suit for Alex and suits for the boys. A friend took a picture of us just as we were about to board the plane. In the picture we look happy and relaxed, but we had to put those smiles on our faces because the Special Branch wanted nothing more than to see that they had got to us. So we walked around with a smile and pretended. Though our hearts were bleeding, we showed them they could not get us down.

We boarded the DC-10 jet and were guided to the rear of the plane where blacks had to sit in those days. We had a two-hour stop-over in Johannesburg before flying to Kenya en route to London. It was only when the plane touched down for refuelling in Nairobi at midnight that I felt safe for the first time. We were out of South African territory.

In the weeks before we left, I'd look at Table Mountain and cry bitterly, wondering when I would see it again. Alex tried to comfort me by saying, 'Never mind. We'll work our way back. We'll return home one day, and you will see Table Mountain again.'

Neither of us could have imagined that it would be almost thirty years before I returned, and that Alex would not return at all.

Chapter 19

'I'm leaving'

When we arrived in London, Alex was given a job by another South African exile, Joel Joffe. A defence lawyer in the Rivonia trial, Joel asked Alex to work as a clerk in his company, Abbey Life Insurance. Though Alex was grateful for the job, it nearly drove him mad. He was not the kind of person to sit behind a desk all day looking at files. Seeing his misery, I said, 'Look, rather than lose your marbles, chuck the job and do what you want.' He quit after a few months and was soon asked by a German radio company to write radio plays about apartheid. He was much happier doing this and kept it up for several months before the ANC asked him to take on unpaid political work as a spokesperson. In the UK it was much easier than in South Africa to inform people about apartheid and to gain their support. Alex was an experienced speaker, so the ANC also sent him abroad, at first only for short trips but later to speak at international conferences.

In the meantime I started work as an auxiliary nurse at the City of London Maternity Hospital in Islington, North London. At first I worked part-time, from eight till three, so that I could spend time with Eugene and Barto when they came home from school. The boys were happy I was not delivering babies in patients' homes, which would have required me to be away at night.

Reg September, who'd been in exile in London for several years, insisted that our family share the house in which he, his wife Hettie and their children Peter and Mark lived in North London. Peter was a few years older than Eugene, and Mark, their younger son, was one year younger than Barto. Hettie and I weren't close friends, but all four of us were members of the ANC and the Coloured People's Congress. When we moved in we arranged to share the household duties. Hettie would do the cooking for both families and I the washing – all by hand since we didn't have a washing machine. Hettie would also look after our boys as well as hers until I returned home from work.

The strain of two families living together in one house got to me. Alex was often abroad, so he didn't feel the tension as the boys and I did. I became terribly frustrated, but I tried to understand that I had moved in on Hettie, encroaching on her space. I felt I had to bend to her wishes; she was under strain, too.

When Alex returned from one of his trips, I asked him to find our own place. He said I had been spoiled living on my own in South Africa and couldn't live with other people. Though he was right to the extent that I didn't fit in well with communal living, I thought he didn't support me. I felt little joy when he told me we'd have to stay there until he had time to resettle the children and me. But he never had time. He was seldom home. He was so involved in travelling as an ambassador for the ANC that he didn't realise he was sacrificing his family to his political work.

Once when he returned from a trip I said, 'Either you stay and see us into a home, or I'm moving out.' He ignored me and went abroad again. I then told the boys that when Daddy came home I would be away for a short while. They had to be patient because we would all benefit from having our own space.

When Alex returned I carried out my threat and took a room at the hospital. 'I'm leaving,' I said. It was the only way I could make him realise he'd have to get his act together and decide what to do. He didn't believe me until I left. I also told him – though I did not carry this out – that I'd report him to the welfare officer.

I think he took heed. He asked me to return home and said he wouldn't go away again until he'd found a house for us. I came back after a week. Yet when we purchased the house, we did so with Reg and Hettie, which didn't solve the problem at all. Alex reminded me that 'as a comrade you should not just think of yourself'. Although we were at loggerheads, for the sake of the children I decided to be satisfied. We had to make do.

○

When a vacancy opened for a six-month refresher course in midwifery I jumped at the opportunity. I was earning only a small income and Alex didn't have a steady salary. Moreover, London was expensive compared to South Africa. My hope was that when I qualified I could get a better position and support the family on my own. Alex would be free to go abroad whenever he was called on by the ANC. Having a tough time in the short run would pay off for us and life would become easier.

While engaged on this course I again had to do home deliveries, day or night. I also had to live in at the hospital and could see Eugene and Barto only on my days off. It was a stressful time for us. I was never sure when Alex would be called by the ANC to travel abroad. I constantly worried about Eugene and Barto, who were having a difficult time adjusting, particularly Barto, who was seven or eight at the time. He was clearly anxious and feeling depressed. The boys missed seeing me and I missed seeing them. I ran away from the hospital several times a week so I could spend an hour or two with them.

In these circumstances I couldn't concentrate on my studies, catch up on writing my case histories, and absorb what I was being taught. The course was intense, and by the fifth of the six months I was ready to leave. I'd packed my bags and was making my way down the stairs when I walked into my Irish friend Nicky. I told her it was over for me. She simply took my bag and escorted me back upstairs to my room. I didn't protest.

'Only one month more, Blanche,' she said. 'Twenty-eight days!'

'No,' I cried. 'It's thirty-one days.'

With her encouragement I completed the course. When I came home, Barto asked me not to go away again. I assured him I would stay home from then on.

○

In London the boys received political instruction, as did many other children of ANC exiles. Once a month on Saturday afternoons Pallo Jordan, who later became arts and culture minister in South Africa, lectured the children on what was happening in South Africa and how the ANC was conducting the Struggle.* Though some of the children were quite young, he brought the lessons down to their level to help them understand clearly what the Struggle was all about and what contribution was expected of them.

Barto grew frustrated with the lectures. 'I don't like Uncle Pallo,' he'd say. 'I don't understand what he's saying.'

'Never mind, Bartie,' Eugene would tell him. '*I* will tell you what he's saying.'

In the meantime Alex and I reinforced at home what Pallo was telling the children in his lectures. It was no good for us to be so involved in the Struggle if the children were only going to be kept aside and 'protected'. The idea imprinted on all of us was that your husband or father or mother wasn't fighting for *your* freedom. Each person must fight for his *own* freedom, including children from an early age. Children must know that life is more than playing and having a good time.

When the boys were in their early teens they made their contribution by typing news briefings for exiles. The news briefing committee was organised by Gill Marcus.† She'd get all the South African English-language newspapers from the South African Embassy side-shop and then clip the articles she thought were important for us exiles to read. On Thursday evenings Eugene and Barto fetched the articles at Gill's office, then typed them on a typewriter she provided. They spent Friday evening and much of Saturday completing their work, which Gill would

---

*   At the time, Jordan was doing postgraduate study at the London School of Economics. By 1975, he worked full-time in information for the ANC in London before moving to Luanda, Angola, in 1977 to head Radio Freedom and Lusaka, Zambia, in 1980 to head the ANC Research Unit. He was born in 1942, the son of the noted scholar Dr A.C. Jordan and Phyllis (Ntantala) Jordan. He matriculated from Athlone High School in Cape Town and joined the ANC while a student at UCT.

†   Gill Marcus is currently Governor of the South African Reserve Bank.

collect at eleven on Sunday morning. She then collated the typed articles into a small booklet and in this way we exiles could stay in touch with what was happening in South Africa.

Gill was meticulous and hard-working. To stay in the office until two in the morning was no problem for her. At first neither Barto nor Eugene could type, but Gill was firm. 'You don't know how to type? Here's a typewriter. Now go and learn.' Until they learned to type with even just two fingers tapping on the keyboard, I did the typing for them. Gill didn't take any excuse for their not having the work ready on time. Her discipline was something the younger generation needed.

Although Eugene and Barto grew up British, we didn't worry about their losing touch with what it meant to be South African. We always had *Sechaba*, the publication of the ANC, in the house. We also had tapes of South African music, especially Kaapse music, because we were quintessentially Capetonians, as well as African songs, to keep them in touch with their cultural roots. Though they eventually lost contact with their friends, we spoke often about my mother and their cousins.

Alex got along well with the boys. He understood them, and he explained things to them. He gave them little cultural lectures, explaining the difference between poetry and prose, or opera and ballet. We had so little money we couldn't afford to go to the cinema often, but when we did go we liked Westerns. While at home Alex was always sitting at the typewriter – an image both boys remember well.*

As in Cape Town, I supported us financially when we lived in London. Alex didn't have a paying job, and I was earning just enough to cover the household bills. We could barely afford the payments on the house.

---

* While in London Alex La Guma published the novels *The Stone Country* (1967) and *In the Fog of the Season's End* (1972), and edited *Apartheid: A Collection of Writings on South African Racism by South Africans* (1971), which included writings by O.R. Tambo, Arthur Nortje, Breyten Breytenbach and Dennis Brutus. La Guma also wrote *A Soviet Journey*, a travel narrative published in Moscow (1978), and his final novel, *Time of the Butcherbird* (1979).

Alex didn't ask me for money because he was quite satisfied with the few pounds the ANC gave him for travel. Though he was running all over the world, he didn't even think to ask the ANC for money to buy a cup of coffee at the airport. He never complained and that was probably a disadvantage. If he had opened his mouth he might have been given something. But he always said, 'The ANC hasn't got the money and you don't take from the Movement.'

Occasionally, if I had any money I'd give it to him. I bought whatever he said he needed, including his cigarettes. He was used to that arrangement. During the last five years in Cape Town he was either under house arrest or detained, so he had no way of earning except for a small advance he might receive for an article or story.

Alex was so unused to spending money that he didn't know how to spend it when he had the chance. Once in London I was too busy to shop, so he did the shopping for me. I think he had £2. 'Buy some vegetables,' I said. 'I need those for a little something tonight.' Alex came back with a tube of toothpaste. 'I noticed we were running short of toothpaste,' he said. He had no idea what to buy or what was a priority.

If Alex had any money, he'd spend it on the boys. On one of the few occasions that he received a royalty, he took the boys to Carnaby Street, one of London's fashion areas, and spent his money buying the boys a shirt or a pair of pants. It was just like him to spend on them and not on himself.

Alex was easy-going and down-to-earth. He couldn't care less about his appearance. I'd sometimes say to him, 'Can't you make yourself look better? You're meeting presidents of other countries. You can't look like this.' He never liked wearing a suit. In fact, I had to trick him into buying a suit. I'd ask him just to try on a suit and afterwards I'd say to the salesman, 'We'll keep it. Give me the bill, please.'

Chapter 20

'Because of South Africa, I felt I was able
to take on anything and succeed'

Having qualified as a nurse-midwife in South Africa, I could start nursing in England without having to take a test. Our nursing standard in South Africa was quite high. To a large degree the South African standard was British to begin with, since British nurses came over to teach us, many from St Thomas' Hospital in London.

I worked as a nurse-midwife in London from 1967 to 1971, receiving a promotion in 1970 from staff nurse to ward sister in charge of a huge lying-in ward for mothers and babies. My employer was a nursing association called the North London Group. Most of the time they worked us to a frazzle. At first I did midwifery house calls as part of my advanced midwifery course, which also involved learning about the British welfare state. I then worked at the City of London Maternity Hospital until I quit, so that I could be home with the boys.

I spoke my mind the entire time I worked as a nurse in England. When a vacancy arose for lying-in ward sister there must have been eighty applications. At first I didn't apply because Matron told us there wasn't much chance for a married woman or one with children to get the job since the hospital needed people there all the time. I had a decent job, I told myself, and in any case I was going home one day. When I left South Africa my mother said to me, 'Never mind. It will be only ten years. The time will go quickly. We will see each other again.'

The secretary came and spoke with me. 'Matron wants to know why you didn't apply for this position.'

'Matron has made it clear that there's no chance of me getting the position,' I said. 'I'm not only married, I've also got children. And I'm not here permanently. I'm going back home someday.'

It seemed she didn't even hear me. 'Matron has asked you to apply.'

I went to Alex. 'What do I do?'

'It won't do you any harm,' he said. 'Apply.'

So I applied. Lo and behold, the advert for the job that had been up on the wall came right off. I'd only been a staff nurse for a year, but I made the interview short-list. Four of us sat waiting to be interviewed by three consultants and Matron. The other nurses were younger than me and very nervous. They were so keen on getting the position, I could see they were all tensed up. But I could relax.

We were asked the same question by Matron and apparently that's where they all fell down. 'What would you do if you find that you're expecting a baby after you've been given this position?'

They all said, 'Have an abortion.'

When my turn came I said, 'I'd be delighted. I haven't had a baby for a long time!'

Barto was quite old at the time, eleven or twelve. I'd always hoped to have a bigger family. As for the job, I told the interview committee that I'd say, 'Thank you very much for offering me the job, but I'm going to have a baby. That's more positive than having a promotion.'

After the interview, while waiting for the result, I ran upstairs because I'd left my ward in charge of a junior nurse. The interviews were taking place down below and I had to check my patients and see how the nurse was coping. But while I was upstairs they called me to come back down.

'How can you just disappear?' Matron asked when I came back in. 'You know you're applying for this position. You're keeping the consultants waiting.'

'I had to go upstairs. I have only one junior nurse with me on the ward, and I wanted to check and see if all was well. I'm sorry. I do apologise if I've left you waiting.'

One of the consultants who favoured me, Mr Donaldson, came to my rescue. 'Sister – oh, I'm sorry, staff nurse,' he said, because I hadn't yet been told I'd been given the job. 'No, I think the staff nurse did the right thing. She's more concerned about the patients than in getting this position.'

After a bit more chatter Matron asked, 'How will you get to work if there's no transport?' I lived about half an hour from the hospital, quite a distance. 'Matron,' I said, 'there's no transport on Christmas Day, but I am here at a quarter to eight because I walk. I've walked before and I'll walk again. I won't let my work suffer just because there isn't a bus.'

'What if your children get sick?' she asked.

'Well, then I'll have to say, "Look, my child is ill. I cannot be at work today." And if it happens too often, I'll resign. My children come first. I'm not going to sacrifice them for this job. My children suffered enough in South Africa. I will not have them suffer again as we did in South Africa.'

I got the job. The other candidates thought there'd been something underhand about the way I got the position. They were younger and inexperienced – I don't mean in nursing, but in life. Because of what I had endured in South Africa, I felt I was able to take on anything and succeed.

As sister-in-charge of the lying-in ward I had to make sure everything was running correctly – that nothing was leaking, that the fire escape worked and so on. My main task, though, was to manage and inspire the nurses. I felt that I got the best out of them. You can only run a ward under strict discipline, but you must be flexible too. You're dealing with patients who can be difficult, and with nurses who can be difficult and who will defy you. Sometimes they would want time off. They'd ask, 'Sister, are you busy tonight?'

'Yes. Look at all this work that has to be done.'

'All right, Sister, we'll stay.'

They knew that come Saturday I'd say, 'You were very nice in helping me the other day. I'm not so busy now; I can cope. Take the day off. I can't pay you out, but maybe this will help.'

Matron couldn't understand how I got them to work the extra time. 'Why are they still here?'

'Because I treat them well,' I said. 'When I need help, they're willing to come. And when there's a chance I can let them go.'

'But that's going against the rules.'

'I'm dealing with human beings,' I said. 'I can't run it in a dogmatic, regimented manner. They're willing to help when I need them. And when I don't, I let them go.'

After a year I resigned the position because I was fed up with what was going on at the hospital. I was hopelessly overworked the entire time. In a photo taken at the time I look terrible – gaunt and thin. At times I felt that rather than make the effort to pour a cup of tea or even drink a cup of water, I'd rather just take the forty winks I needed so badly.

The Matron and I also had a terrible fallout. I grew frustrated because we were understaffed, and I certainly couldn't do the work all on my own. Matron would schedule only four training nurses to work with me, and quite often these nurses had been instructed by her to attend their training lectures. Sometimes I had a qualified staff nurse with me, yet even she would be taken from me to work in another ward, leaving me as the only qualified nurse on duty. That really made my blood boil.

In addition, Matron came walking around like a big boss, reprimanding me: 'Sister! This bed isn't made yet.'

'No, Matron, it isn't,' I'd say. 'Just roll up your sleeves and help me make the bed.' The Matron called me down to her office.

'That's not the way to speak to me,' she said.

'Matron, are you doing this capably?' I asked. 'I know the nurses must go to lectures, but if they all go to the lecture at the same time I'm left on my own.'

Nurses are usually afraid of confronting the Matron of the hospital. She is, after all, the head of nursing in the hospital, and can make life very difficult for the nurse who challenges her. In most cases the Matron's word will be accepted and the nurse who is reported can be dismissed and her future jeopardised.

But in this case it wasn't just a matter of insubordination. I was concerned about the safety and health of the mothers and their babies. I thought the whole situation had become impossible, so I decided to give notice that I was quitting. I told Alex, 'I'm giving notice in October so I can leave no later than the beginning of November.'

Alex sat typing something and then handed me what he had typed. 'Don't read this,' he said. 'Just take it.'

'I can't.'

'Just take it.'

Well, of course I ignored him and read the letter. He'd written a letter of resignation for me, but dated a month earlier than I'd planned.

'I could never imagine you fighting with the Matron the way you did,' he said. 'It never happened in South Africa.' He was afraid I'd come to the point where I was outrageously rude to the Matron.

I gave my resignation to Matron's assistant, because Matron wasn't there. When she came back from holiday she saw me on the ward.

'I believe you've resigned,' she said.

'Yes, Matron. I have resigned. I've given a month's notice.'

'Well,' she said, 'I'm not accepting it.'

I almost said, 'Ah! You're going to keep me to exploit me even further.' But I shut up, even though I was really annoyed with her. Instead, I asked for an appointment to see her.

When we met in her office she again said, 'I'm not accepting your resignation. You didn't give it to *me*.'

I said, 'Matron, if you have an incompetent assistant who cannot take my resignation, then you have no right to go on holiday.'

'How dare you talk like this!'

'Matron, how dare you refuse to take my resignation. And in any case,' I said, 'I am not working for *you*. I am working for the North London Group, and it is to them that I am tendering my resignation, not to you. They will provide you with another person you can push around. I'm not having it.'

'Yes, you people come here from South Africa—'

'Yes, I'm from South Africa. But I've come to do a job here. Tell me anything about my work. *Nothing* went wrong on my wards.'

'Well, I'll hold back your salary.'

She'd adopted a bullying attitude and thought I was afraid of her. But she didn't know I'd been through the mill in South Africa and had defied the Special Branch, and so had no qualms about defying her. I had learned a lot from my lawyers, Himie Bernadt, Henry Brown and Albie Sachs. I knew my rights. I knew how to stand up for myself against those trying to exploit me and defend my dignity. I was prepared to lose my job in defence of my dignity, just as my father had.

When I told Alex how I'd spoken to Matron, he said, 'I think I'm taking you with me to get my award.'

Alex had just won the Afro-Asian Writers' Association Lotus Award for literature. He was deeply involved in the organisation, travelling to various international conferences and serving as deputy secretary-general and later as secretary-general until his death in 1985. He was to be presented with the award by Mrs Indira Gandhi in India, where the Writers' Association conference would be held.

No one at the hospital knew I was married to a famous author. In fact I never mentioned that Alex was an author until one of the doctors met a white colleague from South Africa who told him about Alex and our life fighting apartheid. I was suddenly elevated in their eyes.

The Assistant Matron told everyone, 'You know, La Guma's husband is an intellectual!' They were impressed not with the man for who he was, but because he was an intellectual. One of the nurses even asked me how I had managed to 'catch an intellectual'. This was typical of the class-conscious attitude of people in England. They didn't understand how I was able to keep Alex. They thought I wasn't good enough for him, that I wasn't in his class. One other thing: Alex wasn't a writer when I met him. He only became a writer and international personality while we were married. The irony is that Alex scorned people who were obsessed about class or intellectual difference.

In any case, the nurses were sorry that I was leaving. At my going-away party they gave me a beautiful travelling bag and a smaller handbag.

'I'm going now to India to see my husband get an award,' I said.

'You're probably all pleased to be getting rid of me.' Though I said it tongue-in-cheek, they seemed to take me seriously.

'No, we're not, Blanche,' they said. 'We're sorry to see you go.'

I got on well with all the nurses. What knocked me for a loop was how my promotion set me apart from them. I had started out as a staff nurse and enjoyed knowing the other nurses as friends. But when I became a nursing sister and was put in charge of the ward, I was told I mustn't go into the staff nurses' room anymore.

'I don't understand,' I said to Alex. 'I was with these girls all the time and now I can't go into their room.'

'As a communist you've been studying this very class system,' he said. 'This is it. You're living it now.'

I then saw the true picture.

○

I resigned not only because I was tired and fed up, but also because my absence from home made it difficult for the boys. When I went through the boys' school books I discovered their school work was suffering. Neither Alex nor I had been at home much and like all children, the boys were watching a lot of television. There wasn't television in South Africa while they grew up and so when they came to England they made up for lost time. I felt guilty for not being around. When I gave up my nursing job I thought I'd just have to jump in and manage without the income. I stayed at home for about six months and got Eugene and Barto in order, and when a job opportunity came up to care for a little disabled boy, I took it. But I never went back to nursing. After twenty years in the profession I stopped nursing completely.

Chapter 21

'It's not propaganda, but information'

In September 1971 I began work as office manager for *Soviet Weekly*, a magazine and information bureau that provided the West with photos and stories in English about news and developments in the republics of the Soviet Union. Its office was in a six-storey house in Kensington.*

I was interviewed for the job by George Kuznetsov, the chief Soviet editor and head of information at the Soviet Embassy. He was happy to discover I was Alex La Guma's wife. They knew that Alex and I were communists who had played a role in the Struggle in South Africa and that as a friend of the Soviet Union I could be counted on to be loyal.

'Blanche, we must have one of our own here,' George said.

'But I can't type,' I admitted.

'I'm not worried about your typing,' he said. 'I want you to work under the manager as sub-manager here. You start tomorrow.'

I started work at *Soviet Weekly* during a time of severe diplomatic strain between Britain and the Soviet Union. Just two days after hiring me, George Kuznetsov was deported on charges of spying, along with many others at the Soviet Embassy.† When he interviewed me, he seemed to know that he and other Embassy staff would soon be leaving the UK. The paranoia of the Cold War apparently made the British

---

* *Soviet Weekly* began as *Soviet War News Weekly*, a publication of the Soviet Information Bureau first produced January 1942 in London. During the Cold War, *Soviet Weekly* evolved into a source of information to the West on Soviet public institutions and life. It continued publication until December 1991, just after the collapse of the Soviet Union.

† On 24 September 1971 the British government expelled 90 Soviet Union representatives and banned the return of 15 others on charges of being spies. Chief among those expelled was Georgi A. Kuznetsov, head of the information section of the Soviet Embassy.

government think that many Russians working at the Embassy were spies. Anti-Russian feeling in the UK was rife at the time.

At *Soviet Weekly* no one talked about the expulsions, or perhaps I was just too new for anyone to tell me what they thought. To my knowledge none of those expelled was told what they had done to make them guilty of spying. All embassies have their spies, of course. I didn't feel bad that I was working for an organisation with spies. After all, I'd been in the anti-apartheid underground in South Africa.

I was the first South African to be employed at *Soviet Weekly*. British Communist Party members also worked there. (All of the Russians employed there spoke some level of English.) The Soviets felt that because of the Cold War they came across in the West as monsters. Their attitude seemed to be, 'Don't be nasty to us; we are not so bad.' Anti-Soviet propaganda was being spread in the West, especially America, and our duty was to show the better part of what happened in the Soviet Union. For example, I don't think there's any better ballet company than the Bolshoi – perhaps some are equal to it, but none better. We also held exhibitions, for example at Earls Court, where we'd have a stall to display Soviet products like wines or crafts.

I always believed in the rightness of what I was doing. I never felt I was being used as part of a propaganda machine. When I gave away copies of *Soviet Weekly* someone would invariably say, 'Oh, you're here with your Soviet propaganda.' I'd reply, 'No sir, you're mistaken. It's not propaganda, but information.' (Occasionally I'd also be called a 'black Soviet', to which I'd reply, 'Yes, and proudly so!')

I went to work willingly with the aim of promoting information about the various republics of the USSR. I never felt the information or photos were too optimistic or positive. Rather, they showed what I was working toward in my own country, South Africa: a job for everyone, bread for all, a roof over people's heads. I'm talking about the philosophy of communism. That is what I wanted and supported. I'm not under the illusion that the way communism played out in the Soviet Union was the same as the ideal. My whole attitude to being a communist is that my purpose is to make a better life for everybody.

People say to me even now, 'Look at what Stalin did.' Yes, Stalin was a real villain. When Eugene studied in Moscow in the late 1970s, he learned about the terror of Stalin. He was no better than Hitler. He killed off all his generals and treated the peasants terribly. But at the time, who knew? It was only later that I learned about the difficulty of the farm workers and the hell they went through. But those photographs of the Holocaust and the Second World War were real. The Russians crushed the Germans, and that was the only way to get rid of Hitler. I believed with every fibre of my being that the war photographs we published helped tell the story of the Soviet Union. The USSR was also the most loyal supporter of the ANC against apartheid and oppression in South Africa.

Soviet Weekly was delivered to vending boxes around Great Britain. Organisations and individuals also had subscriptions. We didn't sell a great amount, but we did sell some. The idea was to get them out cheaply through the widest possible distribution. One of our bigger problems was that our vending boxes were often vandalised – blown up and burnt, or the papers were stolen –sometimes by members of the fascist National Front, which also sent us nasty letters. But we never laid a charge. We just replaced or repaired the property. This was the time of the Cold War and such incidents were to be expected. We also received nasty phone calls, though we never knew who called.

My job was largely to see that subscriptions were properly dispatched by rail to the whole of the UK. I also had to make sure the building we worked in didn't fall apart. The entire six-storey building was Soviet property. I went up and down those storeys all the time, checking fire escapes and making sure the building was in sound shape. I also had to see to the paper supply and the stationery. I worked carefully with a budget so that at the end of the day if we were short of something I had enough money to buy it. My experience as ward sister in a hospital helped in all this. The only difference was that now instead of ordering medicines I was ordering pencils and pens.

Sometimes the Soviet way of doing things frustrated me. It was quite bureaucratic. At one point we needed a typewriter. I had exceeded the budget for typewriters but had plenty of money left for stationery. I said to my boss, 'You know, we've gone £200 over, but we need a typewriter. Can't I buy one?'

'Nyet, Blanche! That's money that you paid out.'

It wasn't just his opinion; it was a Soviet ruling. They were terribly inflexible. So of course I said, 'What the heck am I going to do with two thousand pencils and one thousand ball-point pens?'

But I did what I was told because I was afraid to do anything else. Once I said to him, 'Look, the typewriter's broken and needs to be repaired. We must have a new typewriter.' But we couldn't sell or even give away the old typewriter because confidential information might have been imprinted on the ribbon and could get into the wrong hands. We had to be extremely cautious. We were dealing with governments that were violently against us and would use anything to try to get us down.

◯

On one occasion I went downstairs to fetch some reams of paper lying in the passage. I was shocked to discover two men in the bathroom. One of them was a chap I recognised from South Africa.

'Coetzee!' I said. 'Good God, what the hell are you doing here?'[*]

He was one of the Special Branch men who'd arrested me years earlier in Cape Town.

'You were at my house,' I said. 'You came to arrest me.'

Coetzee recognised me but said nothing.

'What the hell are you doing here?' I repeated. 'You've got no right to be here. This is Soviet property.'

They said they were doing a plumbing job.

'You've not come to do a plumbing job,' I said. 'Since when are you a plumber?'

I went on and on. I wasn't scared at all. But they were gone in two ticks. I'm sure these men were planting bugs in the bathroom. The other man was British and lived next door. I was told by one of my British colleagues that this man had been a general in the British Army during

---

[*]   Johann Coetzee along with Craig Williamson ran 'the European spy network' for the Special Branch in the 1970s and 1980s.

the Second World War. It was he, apparently, who brought Coetzee into the building, which was thought to be secure.

When I spoke with British Communist Party people at *Soviet Weekly* about the incident, they had no clue that these men might be spies. They hadn't been part of the Struggle in South Africa and thus had no experience of how these men worked. Ron Harding, the English editor, told me he didn't think the men were spies. He said I was being paranoid and making a fuss over nothing.

But London was overflowing with South African spies working for the Special Branch. In fact, the South African Embassy was full of spies. They had a vast force planting bugs all over. We exiles actually knew some of these Special Branch men from back home. Our Jo'burg people recognised the ones who had operated in Jo'burg, and we Capetonians knew the ones from Cape Town. We saw them at demonstrations, including some of the very men who arrested me and Alex at our house in 1963. They also came to our anti-apartheid meetings pretending they were insiders and members of the ANC. We found out afterwards that top people in the Special Branch had infiltrated us – Craig Williamson, for example, was a double agent working simultaneously for the ANC and the apartheid regime. He was responsible for blowing up our ANC office in London after he'd killed Ruth First in Mozambique.[*]

Soviet Weekly paid well. Though it was enough for me, it wasn't enough to feed a husband and two children. I took a second job doing extra hours at the London Clinic, a private hospital. I worked from nine to five at *Soviet Weekly* and from five thirty to ten at the clinic. I wasn't a nurse but a domiciliary, serving food to the patients. I worked at both jobs for six months until I collapsed with pneumonia. The doctor put me on antibiotics and told me I had to give up the second job. At first I resisted. But I had worked myself to the point of exhaustion, and finally was forced to give up the second job for the sake of my health.

---

[*] Craig Michael Williamson, a former South African police major, was involved in a series of state-sponsored overseas bombings, burglaries, kidnappings, assassinations and propaganda. The TRC granted amnesty to Williamson for the killing of Ruth First and Jeanette and Katryn Schoon and to Williamson and seven others for bombing the London office of the ANC in March 1982.

Chapter 22

'The juice in that orange is the blood of the African worker'

One of the main aims of the ANC in London was to inform the people of Britain and beyond about what was happening in South Africa. To this end, we held regular meetings which helped keep the exiled family together. Since ANC people didn't live in the same area, there were ANC branches in different parts of the city. After branch meetings we'd all get together at a main meeting and discuss ideas for action. Getting to those larger meetings wasn't always easy, and we didn't have much money for train fare. When Alex and I went to the meetings, Barto, who was then a young teenager, complained that he too wanted to take part. So we arranged for Alex to attend all of the meetings since he was the local chairman, and the boys and I would take turns in going with him. Whenever there was a large demonstration we would all go, for example to protest for the release of Nelson Mandela.

When Alex arrived in London he immediately spoke out within the ANC about the lack of accountability to headquarters in Lusaka. Everybody was just doing his own thing. 'Who does what? How much money was made at such-and-such an event? Where is all this information?' Alex asked. He also helped heal a potential rift between the Coloured People's Congress (CPC) and the ANC. In March 1966, just a few months before we left South Africa, Barney Desai and Cardiff Marney, president and chairman respectively of the CPC in exile in London, issued a statement that severed the CPC's ties with the ANC, dissolved the CPC, and announced that it had merged with the Pan Africanist Congress (PAC). This was definitely not the case. Back in

Cape Town, Alex sent out messages to inform CPC members about Desai's false announcement and ask their opinion about continuing the CPC. When he arrived in London, he led the efforts to reaffirm the CPC's longstanding ties to the ANC.*

While based in London, Alex travelled for the ANC both within and outside the country to talk about the Struggle in South Africa. He was asked to speak, for example, to the Anti-Apartheid Movement at Oxford and to the large Anti-Apartheid Movement in Holland, which paid his fare for a weekend visit. Whenever Reg September was asked by the BBC for a South African to interview, he'd suggest Alex.† Alex was a roaming ambassador, free to go whenever he was called upon. He was away all the time. But I did my part, too: I stayed home and worked.

All London members of the ANC and the South African Communist Party (SACP) were instructed by the ANC to join the Anti-Apartheid Movement (AAM). AAM was a British organisation that supported the ANC by mobilising the British public against apartheid. More than this, the AAM was the centre of the international movement against apartheid. Anti-apartheid movements were established in many European countries, the British and Dutch being the largest. These movements eventually brought about sanctions against South Africa, which helped to topple the regime.

The AAM deserves high praise for all the work it did to assist in the Struggle against apartheid. The relationship between the ANC and AAM was close, and only when we arrived in London did we become aware of the British AAM's enormous support. We were instructed by

---

* Desai was angered when his application for membership of the ANC was rejected on the grounds that the ANC was open only to black Africans. The Congress Alliance convened a meeting in November 1966 and appointed Alex La Guma to a recommendations committee. In his report, La Guma – acting as main representative of the CPC – repudiated the affiliation of the CPC and PAC and reaffirmed the Congress Alliance stance that the ANC was the leader of the struggle.

† Reg September served as the chief representative of the ANC in London and Western Europe from 1965 to 1978. He was then deployed to Lusaka to serve on the ANC's revolutionary council.

the ANC to join the AAM but not run the show. Sometimes we couldn't help it. Where we lived in Muswell Hill there was no AAM branch. Our good friends Fred and Sarah Carneson lived one neighbourhood away in East Finchley. The four of us reckoned that as we didn't have an AAM Muswell Hill branch, we should start one. The participants at the first meeting were Fred, Sarah, Alex and Blanche. Then we realised AAM was not an ANC organisation. We first had to find a British person to run the organisation before we could join. It was quite funny.

One of the key tactics of the AAM was to boycott consumer goods from South Africa, including fruit. I remember once being in a food store when a British woman sang to me the praises of South African fruit. She compared our fruit with those from France and Spain, telling me South African fruit was much better – sweeter and cheaper. 'These oranges are the best,' she said, holding up one. I looked at her and spoke my mind.

'You know what you are buying with those South African oranges? The juice in that orange is the blood of the African worker.'

'Are you serious?'

'Yes, I am,' I said. 'Black people are suffering terribly while you eat the fruit which you say is so good. It's *not* good.'

Many Brits argued that South African blacks would suffer under a boycott. But the fact is that South African blacks were already suffering and had asked for the boycott. We felt the British should do what the people at home were asking. In general, the boycott was more effective when it was led by a British group like AAM than by us because the Brits could influence their own people. But in the instance just mentioned, I just had to let the woman know what she was getting when she bought a South African orange.

○

The International Defence and Aid Fund for Southern Africa (IDAF) was another huge help to us. I was both a donor and recipient of IDAF aid. Defence and Aid began during the Treason Trial in 1956 when money was needed to pay for the defence of trialists like Alex and for aid to their dependants. When funds raised within South Africa proved not enough, Canon John Collins of St Paul's Cathedral in London came to the rescue and campaigned for international assistance on humanitarian grounds. Some European countries knew what it was like to live under the Nazis during the Second World War and thus could make the connection with our struggle against fascism. Eventually IDAF was formed and supported us throughout. Defence and Aid was separate from, but related to, the AAM, as many who were active in the AAM also supported IDAF.*

Defence and Aid was especially helpful in assisting those in dire need, like the large families of liberation movement members whose welfare grant from the state was not enough to feed everyone. IDAF also helped with smaller practical matters. Once I needed to replace my spectacles but couldn't afford new ones. I was advised by the ANC to request assistance from Defence and Aid. I took the cheapest frame I could find. When I walked into the ANC office, Solly Smith, ANC chief representative in the UK, asked me why I had bought such an ugly frame. He said he'd paid £100 for his frame with a grant from IDAF. I told him I thought he was unscrupulous to exploit an organisation that was helping the needy. After all, the lens – not the frame – was the important part.

Some of our ANC people worked closely with Canon Collins, among them Rica Hodgson. She asked me to correspond with and provide financial support to Gladys Marks, the wife of SACP chairman J.B. Marks, whom we fondly called Uncle J.B. I corresponded with her in Johannesburg for more than ten years, beginning shortly after my arrival in 1966. IDAF would send me an international money order, which I would then include in my letter to Gladys. I'm not sure where the money came from, because that was kept secret. I was also not to tell

---

* The International Defense and Aid Fund for Southern Africa (IDAF) was founded by Canon John Collins of St Paul's Cathedral, London. Beginning with the Treason Trial in 1956, the London-based organisation smuggled £100 million into South Africa for the defence of thousands of political activists. Hundreds of letter writers from Britain, Scandinavia, Holland, Ireland and Canada sent IDAF money through the post to 'pen-pals' in South Africa and kept quiet about it for years.

anybody where the money order was going, as that would be dangerous. The Special Branch might open the letter and find the money, and then would put a stop to it.

The correspondence with Gladys had to be simple and innocent: 'I hope you're keeping well. The children are fine. I'm very well, etc. I had a little windfall' or 'I did very well at work. I got a bonus, and I thought I'd share it with you.' She would thank me for the gift, write about the weather, say they were keeping well, and ask me about myself and my family. I put a false return address on the envelope and left off my name. When I received her reply, I'd give it to Rica to pass on to Canon Collins and his committee. If I didn't receive a letter from Gladys, that meant she wasn't getting the money, so nothing more would be sent. It was imperative that she let me know she had got it. In her letter she wouldn't mention money, but rather say, 'I received your letter of the 13th and thank you for the gift.' She also couldn't write directly about political problems, but might be able to signal something. She'd mention that the cost of living had gone up, meaning that she needed additional funds,

Blanche (left) protesting outside South Africa House in London, 1977

information that I would pass on to Defence and Aid.

I also corresponded with and supported James April, who was serving fifteen years on Robben Island for his activities as an MK soldier. When Alex and I later left for Cuba, his sister Helen April took over the task of corresponding with James from London. At one point James wrote to her to say he was interested in learning to play the guitar, so I sent IDAF money through her to enable him to buy an instrument. Though the prison authorities censored some of the prisoners' letters on Robben Island, they allowed James to acquire a guitar.

James April was one of two young coloured men from Cape Town who were almost like sons to Alex. The other was Basil February. The two were political twins. They were young intellectuals of the Unity Movement whom we first met in the early 1960s. James and Basil would have heated debates with Alex into the early hours of the morning. Since the Unity Movement really didn't do anything to oppose the government, these young men had become increasingly frustrated. At first Alex's discussions with James and Basil weren't persuasive enough to make them realise that the only way to bring the regime to its knees was by the armed struggle.

One evening Alex came to me looking very sad.

'You know, I've lost the battle,' he said. Alex never lost a political debate with anyone. He always came out on top with the right answers and the right way of debating. But he felt he'd lost with those young men. He just could not influence them.

Alex was then put under house arrest. When he next spoke with James and Basil he could do so only over the fence in his mother's yard.

One evening they came to say goodbye. They didn't say where they were going, because in those days you just did not. Alex wept because he knew they had in fact joined Umkhonto we Sizwe (MK) and were leaving the country to go to an MK camp in Zambia. MK had arranged for them to join their comrades outside the country.

'I haven't lost, you know,' Alex said to me. 'I'm sure they're going. They're not supposed to say, but they've come to say goodbye.'

'I told you that you hadn't lost the battle,' I said.

After James and Basil had left, nobody knew where they were, not even their families. James had been living with his mother in Bokmakierie, a council estate in Athlone, which later became Hazendal. When I visited my patients in Bokmakierie, James's mother would come to the gate and say to me, 'Nurse, where is my Jamesie? *You* know where my Jamesie is.' Well, I had an idea – I knew he had left the country – but it wasn't for me to say.

When we arrived in England two years later in 1966, the ANC arranged for Reg and Alex to visit ANC headquarters and the MK camp in Zambia. When Alex arrived at the camp the commander in charge said, 'Alex, I want you to meet your two sons.' He was taken to James April and Basil February, the young men from Cape Town whom he'd recruited into Umkhonto we Sizwe.

The next year Basil February was killed in Rhodesia. He was part of the Wankie campaign in which MK soldiers tried to make their way through Rhodesia into South Africa. I spoke with Basil's brother, who told me what a terrible death it was. Basil had bravely fought to the death against the Rhodesian and South African soldiers. They hung his body on a post and paraded it around. When the police informed his parents they gloated, 'We've killed the pig.' People will never understand how vicious these people were. But Alex knew, and he never forgot. In 1972 he dedicated his novel *In the Fog of the Season's End* to Basil February.

James April was also part of the Wankie campaign. He was caught and served eighteen months in prison in Botswana. In 1971 he was rearrested in South Africa during an underground operation and found guilty on three charges of terrorism. He served fifteen years before being released in 1986.

When I think back to that whole episode and to the sacrifices James and Basil made, it brings tears to my eyes.

Chapter 23

'Don't you think you should stop this marriage?'

Our situation in exile required Eugene and Barto to get on their feet by passing their British A-level exams and going on to university. Alex didn't push them, but instead mentored and encouraged them. They were both bright boys with the potential for university education, but we had no money to pay for the universities in London. After Eugene passed his A-levels in 1975 he chose to go to Moscow and study history. The Russians were the first to offer free tertiary education to our sons. Eugene first had to learn Russian within a year. It was a matter of learn the language and learn fast. There was no playing around.

Barto went to study in East Germany under the same arrangement. After he completed his A-levels, he was given a scholarship to study in Leipzig in the German Democratic Republic (East Germany) in 1978. There he learned the German language and photography. In 1981 he transferred to Potsdam to study cinematography. On completion of his degree in 1985, he went to work at ANC headquarters in Tanzania.

Eugene's time in the Soviet Union was eventful, to say the least. After a year of language study, he enrolled in the Patrice Lumumba University in Moscow.* Mainly foreign students attended the university, but there were some Russians as well. There he met his future wife, Elena Chelnikov, whom we call Lena. Unfortunately, Eugene and two other ANC students, Phaki Nokwe and Ike Nzo, ran foul of the university because of indiscipline. It's never been clear to me what they did, but

* The Patrice Lumumba Peoples' Friendship University was founded in 1960 with the objective of helping Third World nations in Asia, Africa and South America at the height of the Cold War by providing higher education and professional training.

cultural differences played a role. The Russians seemed to emphasise discipline over learning, while the ANC students grew up with the idea that they could challenge their teachers.[*]

○

Prior to leaving Moscow in 1978 and returning to London, Eugene spoke with Sergei Chelnikov, Lena's father, about his intention to marry Lena. Sergei was a captain in the Soviet Army. Because of the Cold War he was not allowed to have foreigners stay at their house, nor could he even meet Eugene, a foreigner, in his uniform, lest there be any suspicion that a Soviet military officer was negotiating with foreigners. So Sergei got into his civilian clothes and they met at a restaurant. Eugene told him that Lena was pregnant and he was prepared to marry her. Knowing this, Sergei decided to quit his military position, which he'd occupied for twenty-five years, to make the marriage possible. When Eugene returned to London he told us about his intention to marry Lena, though he said nothing about her pregnancy.

In June 1978, while working at *Soviet Weekly* in London, I received a call from Alex. He informed me that the ANC executive in Lusaka had unanimously elected him to be the ANC's chief representative to Cuba and the Caribbean. He would be based in Havana for the purpose of informing people in Cuba, Latin America and the Caribbean about the situation in South Africa and the role of the ANC in fighting apartheid. He asked me what I thought about the offer.

'You are a committed member of the ANC,' I said. 'You have to take it, even if they send you to the desert. You'll have to go where you are needed for the Movement.'

When I got home that evening, I was proud and ready to go to Cuba. I assumed I would be joining him until he said to me, 'But you haven't been invited. *I* have been.'

Though it was certain I would go with him, you didn't ever take things for granted in the Movement and you certainly didn't decide

---

[*]   Ike Nzo went on to become a psychiatrist in Gauteng whose work included treating the trauma of crime victims.

where you were going. It was unlikely that the Movement would split up the family, though they might have needed me in another place. As it turned out, after Alex accepted the position they said I would be accompanying him as a sort of second-in-command. I appreciated this. After all, I also worked for the Movement in my own right. I wasn't just an appendage of Alex.

I was excited to go. Cuba was a new area to work in and rather far away. We would have to make decisions on our own. We wouldn't be able to call headquarters and ask, 'What now?' We would also be the first ANC representatives in that area of the world. Cuba was important at the time – not only Cuba, but indeed the whole of Latin America and the Caribbean. Cuba was then lending its support to African liberation movements in Angola, Mozambique, Zimbabwe and South Africa, as well as movements throughout Latin America fighting oppressive regimes. Not only would the Cuban government allow the ANC to open a mission in the country, but it would also support the mission fully. While there, we would be guests of Fidel Castro's government.

Having put down roots in London for twelve years, I needed some time before uprooting and going to Cuba. Alex left in September 1978. I stayed in London for three months tying up loose ends, paying bills and taking care of details regarding the house, which was being let.

Blanche (right) with Alex and other Lotus Award winners, New Delhi, 1970

Before heading off to Cuba, Alex travelled to Moscow for several days. One Saturday he called me.

'Congratulations, Granny,' he said. 'James La Guma the Second has been born.'

Alex had just visited Lena, who had given birth several days earlier in Moscow.

The birth took me completely by surprise. Eugene was with me in London and we cried at the news. He said that he meant to tell me that Lena was pregnant. I congratulated him and said that I welcomed my grandson and that the event called for rejoicing. Lena had named the baby James after reading about the life of Alex's father.

While Eugene and I were sitting there, Sonia Bunting, Brian's wife, phoned to tell me something about the ANC women's section.

I said to her, 'Oh by the way, James La Guma the Second has been born.'

She put the phone down. No doubt she was shocked, thinking, 'Oh Lord, they are now really in with the Soviets rather than us.' Not a minute after we'd finished our call she phoned back.

'Oh, may I please speak with Eugene?'

He didn't want to talk with her. He knew how she'd reacted.

'He's not here,' I said.

'Then give him our congratulations.'

That night the ANC Youth League had a fundraising party. I said to Eugene, 'Go to the party. You'll probably be there among your friends. Get this off your mind.' I gave him some money to celebrate. It was hard on him with Lena and the baby in Moscow while he was in London, and it probably wasn't easy to deal with the fact that he hadn't told me, either.

Some time later in 1978 there was a farewell party for Reg September, who was relocating to ANC headquarters in Lusaka, Zambia. Alex was master of ceremonies. While I was speaking with Brian Bunting, Eugene passed us and I said, 'Oh, that's my son, you know. He's going to give me a daughter' – meaning, of course, that he was preparing to marry Lena Chelnikov.

Brian said to me, 'And don't you think you should stop this marriage?'

'Why? Why can't they get married?'

'The Russians don't like their people, especially their women, to marry foreigners.'

'I've never heard of that,' I said.

'No, Eugene shouldn't marry her,' Brian said. In fact, he said, the marriage should be stopped and Alex and I should be the ones to stop it.

It was such a blow to hear this. He and others in the ANC must have been discussing the matter. Brian even told me to contact Vladimir Shubin in Moscow and ask him to stop the marriage. (I never did.)[*]

The pressure only got worse. The top brass of the South African Communist Party (SACP), Brian Bunting and Dr Yusuf Dadoo, the chairman, went so far as to send one of their members, Herbie Pillay, to speak with me. Herbie said that at one stage he'd attended a youth festival in East Germany and had fallen in love with a German girl. Dr Dadoo told Herbie he shouldn't get involved with this girl because it was not acceptable for a foreigner to marry a citizen of the GDR. Herbie broke up with her and now felt it his duty to persuade me to have Eugene put a stop to his marriage to Lena. Perhaps they seriously believed it wasn't acceptable in the Soviet Union. But it didn't work like that with Eugene. Once he'd said to me, 'How can you fall in love and just turn off your affection and your emotions because it's not allowed to happen?'

Now I told Herbie, 'Don't come and interfere in somebody else's life.'

Sometime later I had another visitor, Stephanie Sachs, Albie's first wife and an SACP member. She also asked me to stop the marriage. But none of this worked. Still, I felt the pressure and thought it was unfair: senior members of the Party should not interfere in the lives of the children of Party members. Some of these children weren't even Party members. The whole affair put a tremendous strain on my family. I went to my boss, Vladimir Dobkin, the Russian editor at the *Soviet Weekly*, and told him the whole story.

---

[*] Vladimir Shubin headed the Afro-Asian Solidarity Council and later was CPSU central committee liaison officer with southern African movements.

'You people are supposed to be communists, without any discrimination,' I said. 'A member of my Party' – I didn't mention names – 'tells me the Soviets don't like their women to marry foreigners. Explain that to me. What is the situation? Can Soviet citizens marry foreigners?'

'We are sick and tired of Party members from other countries telling us what our policy is,' Dobkin said. The Communist Party of the Soviet Union did in fact have a policy that their people should not marry foreigners, but it depended on who that person was. In this case there was no problem at all. The Soviet Union knew the La Guma family well. 'We have no objection to the marriage,' he said. It was not up to the South African Communist Party to interpret policy and make the decision for the Soviets. He told me he was going to lunch at the Soviet Embassy and would explain the situation to the Soviet ambassador. 'We'll see what happens,' he said.

The situation was resolved when Alex met with officials during one of his visits to Moscow for a meeting of the Soviet Union Writers' Union. He learned fairly quickly through informal talks outside the meeting that Party officials were fed up with South African communists' involvement in the marriage. SACP members had apparently done what Brian had asked me to do: they went to Vladimir Shubin, hoping he could get Eugene's marriage stopped.

A member of the Politburo asked Alex, 'Do you mind if Eugene marries a Russian girl?'

'It is for these two people to decide,' Alex said. 'They are both adults.'

The Politburo member then told Alex it was agreed that Eugene could come back into the country to marry Lena.

I had a similar conversation with a Russian official, who asked, 'How do you like Lena? Are you happy?'

'It's not for me to say. I'm not the one marrying her,' I said. 'They're sensible adults. If they choose to be married, she's welcome into our family. But it's entirely their decision, if you're going to allow this.'

'Yes, we'll allow this,' he said. 'Blanche, we give our daughter into your hands.'

In the final analysis, the marriage of Eugene and Lena was sanctioned by the Communist Party of the Soviet Union. Brian Bunting and the SACP were right in the sense that Russians wouldn't accept foreigners marrying their own people. It seemed also to be a policy of other socialist countries as well, because a similar thing happened with Barto in the GDR. When Barto wanted to marry Karin, the government wouldn't allow their marriage because Barto was a foreigner. Barto and Karin had to wait for the fall of the Berlin Wall before they could get married. But it was different with Eugene, largely because of Alex's high profile in the Soviet Union and the advantage of the groom's father being an ardent communist who was known in the higher echelons of the Party.

The marriage of Eugene and Lena took place in a state court in Moscow in January 1979. After everything that had happened, I couldn't even go to the wedding because by that time I was on my way to join Alex in Cuba. He had sent letters and telegrams that said, 'Please come over quickly now, because I'm missing you terribly. The Movement needs you, but I also need you.' I felt, 'Well, Eugene is now settled. He's standing on his feet and marrying this girl. It's Alex who needs me.' And so I went to Cuba.

Chapter 24

'It was the happiest time of my life – and Alex's'

I arrived in Cuba on a hot day, just before Christmas. After the cold winter I had just left in London, the tropical sun shone bright and strong over the island. Alex was eagerly waiting for me. By then he had learned to say 'Companera', or comrade. He was so glad to see me that all he could say was, 'Companera! Companera!' Then in English he said, 'My comrade has come to see me.'

He took me to our house, which was also the ANC mission, arranged for us by the Cuban government. The house was located in a western suburb of Havana called Atabey, not far from Fifth Avenue, which ran along the coast into central Havana, with hotels on the opposite side of the road. The area was set aside for missions of national liberation organisations, next to the area for embassies. We lived among Cuban families who were friendly and helpful and with whom we could practise our Spanish. Along with other foreign ambassadors, representatives and embassy personnel, we attended Spanish classes two or three times a week for six months. I could never say the Spanish *n* – that was a big battle for me.

The house sat on a large plot of land (about 750 square metres), including a large back garden, with mango, banana and paw-paw trees – all fruit bearing – and lots of lawn. We planted flowers and flower-bearing trees, as well as roses. It was a solid house, built well above street level to prevent flooding during the tropical rainy season. We used the only room on the upper level as the ANC office.

The Cuban government financed the ANC mission, giving us a monthly stipend in Cuban pesos to pay the rent and telephone and to buy food at a special shop near our home. Most of the food staples were rationed and subsidised. But we could also buy food at other shops not under the rationing system, paying the normal price. The Cubans also gave us a US dollar stipend for purchases at a special foreign currency shop used by the embassies. The stipend wasn't in hard cash but in coupons, which couldn't be carried over from month to month. As we were living in a socialist country, the idea was to use the stipend and not salt the dollars away like a capitalist, building up money for our own use. With the stipend I could buy foodstuffs and little luxuries like chocolates, imported clothes and good fish. The shop also had some of the best fish, like the wonderful crayfish I used in my paella. Curry was hard to come by, so we got that from our ANC representative in Canada, Yusuf Salojee, who would come down at Christmas time and bring me ingredients for curry and other dishes – coriander seed, cinnamon sticks, cloves, and so forth.

For transport the Cuba government gave us a Soviet-made Lada, sturdy, easy to drive, and fully maintained. As Cuba didn't produce cars, they imported them from the Soviet Union. The government also provided Ladas to representatives of other liberation movements, such as Swapo (South West Africa People's Organisation) and Zapu (Zimbabwe African People's Union). The Cubans operated a special garage for these cars, which I found very dependable. As there was a shortage of petrol, Cubans bought petrol through coupons organised by the Communist Party. I always had more than I could use. When I took them back they'd say, 'Why do you come back with the coupons? Why don't you use them? They're given so you can drive around and see our country.' I didn't have the heart, because I thought they were giving us so much already. I'd just use the car for work and occasionally when I'd go out.

We in the liberation movements were all poor people living on the island, and yet the Cuban authorities gave us everything. Cuba had a deep feeling for countries that were oppressed, and they expressed this in what they gave. One wondered how they could share with us when they were struggling economically with their own shortages. If I were ever to go back I'd say, 'Viva Cuba!' and 'Viva Fidel!' They were marvellous.

○

We were not ambassadors of an established government, but a mission providing information to other liberation movements in the region about apartheid and the ANC's role in the fight for liberation. While Cuba was our base, we also worked with other Latin American and Caribbean countries, hoping to receive their support, including, if possible, funding. We also gave support to other liberation movements. Some of the countries were quite poor and could not support us financially even though they supported us politically. During our time in Cuba, Alex travelled frequently throughout the world to speak about apartheid at conferences and meetings. While he was away I held the fort at the mission.

The Cuban authorities asked us many questions because they and the Cuban people weren't fully aware of what was happening inside South Africa. Alex periodically briefed officials assigned to us. The first person put in charge of us was Comrade Vernier, a member of the Cuban Communist Party. He took care of everything for us, seeing that all our needs were met. When he was promoted to a higher position, Comrade Angel Delmau took over. Comrade Delmau was later the first Cuban ambassador to the newly democratic South Africa.

Each month we posted the ANC journal *Sechaba* and *The African Communist* to all liberation movements in the region. Both were written in London, printed and paid for by the German Democratic Republic, and sent to us in bulk. We expanded our international mailing list to such an extent that eventually we had to mail two issues of *Sechaba* together on a bi-monthly basis. (*The African Communist* was published quarterly.) We also gave each ANC student in Havana a copy of both journals and mailed copies to the students in other provinces. I paid for all postage out of our monthly stipend. As we had no envelopes, I made my own by cutting and folding brown paper bought at the foreign currency shop where I also obtained stationery and typewriter ribbons. Though it was time-consuming, I had to do it that way.

Cuban organisations sponsored commemorative events for us on special dates on the ANC calendar, such as 8 January (the ANC's founding), 21 March (Human Rights Day – the Sharpeville Massacre) and 9 August (Women's Day). The Cubans arranged the venue and organised snacks and soft drinks for the event. We had full, receptive audiences of perhaps several hundred including people from the liberation movements as well as ordinary Cubans. Alex spoke or, if he wasn't there, I did. I always spoke on South African Women's Day. If there was a student available who'd been part of the 1976 Soweto Uprising, then he would speak on Youth Day. I'd speak in Spanish, writing out my speech in English, then read from a translation by a Cuban woman. I'd take questions through an interpreter. It was a long process, but nothing was too much for the Cubans to arrange.

We were invited to all Cuban government receptions and to most receptions given by foreign ambassadors celebrating their national days. In the week leading up to 1 January, the day on which Cuba won its liberation in 1959, the Cuban government and other organisations sent us huge baskets of local products, such as fish, shellfish, cheese, fruit, sweets and bottles of Cuban rum.

We met Fidel Castro briefly at various functions. He would stand in front of the receiving line and shake everybody's hand. The first time I met him he said, 'You are from South Africa. I hope you and Alex enjoy your stay in our country.' He knew who I was and why I was there. I was impressed. In fact, before Mandela was released I felt Fidel was the man of the moment, internationally. He stood out in my mind as an icon of the whole international struggle for liberation.

One Sunday each year ICAP (Instituto Cubana de Amistad con los Pueblos – the Cuban Institute of Friendship among People) arranged for all embassy and liberation movement personnel to go to the fields to help harvest the citrus fruit, mainly oranges and clementines and sometimes tomatoes. We'd leave at six in the morning in buses and spend a pleasant day in the fields, taking tea at ten o'clock and having sandwiches and soft drinks at lunch-time. After lunch we would call it a day, because by then we'd worked almost seven hours and it might be getting hot.

We weren't working with farm labourers but only with each other. The farm managers instructed us on how to pick the fruit. For example, if you pull a clementine from the stem (we call them *naartjies* in South Africa) you take off the skin, so you must twist it off. We didn't work just for the benefit of the cultural experience – the Cubans really needed the help. I worked on harvest day every year. If one wanted, one could decline to work: the Cubans didn't mind and many foreigners did decline. But we worked because we were in solidarity with Cuba.

Sometimes worker brigades from other countries joined us in the harvest, paying their own fares to come to Cuba. These brigades usually included students. During lunch or a work break, the Cuban government arranged for representatives from the ANC, Swapo, and Frelimo (Front for the Liberation of Mozambique) to speak to these foreign brigades about the situation in our home countries. Alex would talk about what the ANC was doing to fight apartheid inside and outside South Africa. After working anywhere from half a day to several days, the brigades would travel around Cuba, hosted by the government.

At one stage a brigade from America came over. I don't think they had travelled directly from the United States but arrived in a roundabout way through another country. They were given our home address and one day a small group of about six or eight of them came to visit. They were all young black women – students or teachers who studied Africa.

Alex, Blanche and members of the diplomatic corps picking fruit in Cuba

Alex spoke and they took notes. Though they knew they had come to the ANC mission, they didn't know who was speaking. After Alex had finished, the leader said, 'Do you mind if we have your name, please?'

'I'm Alex La Guma.'

The poor woman asked him, 'Al-lex Lah Goo-mah?' Just like that. She said his name slowly and with emphasis about six times: she couldn't stop. Alex eventually said, 'Well, that's what they call me.'

She was just stunned. She had read all Alex's books but didn't know she'd been speaking with the author.

After the last time she repeated his name I jumped up and said, 'Now will you enjoy a cup of coffee with us?'

○

Living in Cuba was both a lonely and a happy time for me. On the one hand I was in a strange country and my Spanish wasn't very good. As friendly as my neighbours were, I couldn't go and sit with them all day. When Alex was away, I was completely alone. Television was difficult to follow, and I couldn't read all day, either. Henry Brown, our lawyer in London, sent us cassettes to teach us Spanish and I listened to them for practice. But sometimes – not always, but occasionally – I felt a bit unsettled. Alex was away too often and for too long.

On the other hand, it was also the happiest time of my life – and Alex's, I'm sure. Friends from various Cuban organisations often came over to see me, such as ICAP, OSPAAAL (Organización de Solidaridad de los Pueblos de Africa, Asia y América Latina – Solidarity Organization of the Peoples of Africa, Asia, and Latin America), and the Federation of Cuban Women. Occasionally the Federation arranged outings to scenic and historical places for wives of liberation movement representatives and ambassadors as well as embassy staff. Most of the embassy wives kept their distance. There was a kind of elitism: 'I am a representative of a sovereign government. You are only from a liberation movement.' I was close only to the Guyanese ambassador's wife, whom I'd invite over for curry and a few drinks of rum while our husbands were away.

Alex and I felt close to the Cubans with whom we associated. They really took care of us. If there was anything we needed, we'd just say the word and they would be there to assist us. They came over quite a lot, too, especially in the mango season. I'd say, 'Come, we're going to eat mangos today. Mangos and coffee!' The mangos just fell off an enormous tree in our garden, juicy and ripe. When they fell while still green, I'd make delicious mango pickles by cutting them up and adding spices.

Alex and I often visited Cubans in their homes, which other non-Cubans didn't often do. In fact, when one of the Cubans invited us to his wedding, we were the only non-Cubans there. My closest friends were my immediate Cuban neighbours, especially my next-door neighbour Cariño and her sister Cookie Gonzalez, who was married to Inocencio. I spent a lot of time with Cariño. She was much younger than me. She (and others) sometimes called me 'Mama', which didn't bother me because it was a term of affection. Cariño was keen that I speak Castilian Spanish – correct Spanish, doing the lisp. She and I would sit in the garden among the lovely fruit trees and chat about Cuba, South Africa, London, and other places I'd been to. She and others were keen to hear what I had to say because they didn't know much about South Africa. They in turn introduced me to the culture of their country: Cuban food, poetry and the rumba, which is such an important part of their culture – children learn to dance it at school. After a while Cuba began to feel like home and the best place for Alex and me to be.

Chapter 25

'I'll never forget the sight of Alex cooking up a big pot of stew'

In the 1976 Soweto Uprising, students rebelled against Afrikaans as the medium of instruction in the schools. The police broke up these peaceful demonstrations by shooting students with live bullets, killing many and injuring more. Protests erupted across South Africa and hundreds of students fled the country for ANC camps in Zambia and Tanzania, wanting to take up arms against the apartheid regime.

The problem for the ANC was what to do with these young people. They all wanted to fight, but ANC president Oliver Tambo insisted that they go to school. He knew the students had to continue studying not only for themselves and their future, but also to make a bigger and better contribution in South Africa when we had won our liberation. Tambo then approached governments friendly to the ANC and asked if they would take the children and train them.

Students were sent all over the world. The Soviet Union was the first to respond to Tambo's call, accepting ANC students like Eugene to study in Moscow. Other socialist countries quickly followed suit: East Germany, Hungary and Poland. To its credit Cuba also took in students, not only at the tertiary level, as did many countries, but also at the primary and secondary levels. Cuba in fact was the only country that accepted primary school students, educating them on the Isle of Youth, a large island about a hundred kilometres south of the Cuban mainland. Formerly called the Isle of Pines, it was where Fidel Castro was detained for two years in the mid-1950s for attempting to overthrow the Batista government.

Older South African students who had already joined MK were sent to Cuba to study. Cuba provided them with school uniforms and casual clothes – mufti, as we call it. Struggling to care for its own people, Cuba shared what little it had with all liberation movements, not only from Africa, but from Asia and Latin America as well. I become emotional when I think of the generosity with which Cuba helped other oppressed countries.

ANC students came to Cuba via the ANC camps in Zambia. They learned Spanish fairly quickly before going to university in Havana and other provinces such as Santiago de Cuba, the seat of the Revolution on the southeast coast. Many students at the tertiary level studied at the Nico Lopez School, where they received political education in Marxist philosophy for up to three years through intensive courses run by the Communist Party of Cuba. The secondary school students, who were aged about fifteen to seventeen, came from various backgrounds. Sometimes we struggled to make them understand what we were saying, even in English, because their schooling was by and large the very poor Bantu education they had received back home.

We had to be parents to many of these young people. It isn't easy to leave your country, especially when you're young. Though you've been given an education and a place to live, it still isn't home. You miss your parents. You are on your own.

Some of the students in Havana came to our mission quite often. We were always open for them to discuss their problems. Before Alex and I arrived, these young people had no adult supervision. When we came we served as a surrogate Dad and Mom. We welcomed the students to the mission and babied them a bit. They needed a shoulder to cry on. In fact, some of them called me 'Mommy', while others called me 'Auntie' and still others 'Comrade'.

Sometimes the students would sit and chat – often about home – until two or three in the morning. Alex could have stopped it but he didn't. He felt the mission should be a home-from-home. We had little privacy, since our bedroom and the lounge were both on the lower floor, but I got used to it after a while.

My only objection was that when we arrived some of the students whose parents were in the upper echelons of the ANC took advantage of the situation. They came to the mission not just to visit but to stay there at weekends. There were six of them, two boys and four girls. Alex had allowed them to stay over before I arrived. I don't know if it was because he was lonely, or because he himself had sons living far away from home in other countries. As children of leaders in the Movement they felt they were entitled to a better living situation than the hundred or so other students.

Though I wasn't upset at first, my frustration built up after a while. I'd find food rations for coffee or other items in Alex's drawer and wonder why. I then discovered it was because they were using up Alex's food rations and so he had to hide them. Other students started to complain that we were discriminating against them. Alex was afraid of being hard on these young people, but I made it clear they couldn't remain.

'Think about the food,' I said.

'Don't get personal,' he responded.

The students also did their washing at the mission, using up all of our soap – also under ration – and turning the place into a real den, hanging clothes outside over the fence as one sees in the townships. 'It looks like a blinking mess,' I complained to Alex. 'People will say in the street, "Where is the ANC mission?" "Oh, it's down there where all that washing is hanging."'

This is where we fell out with the students. They couldn't understand my attitude, which they considered my *English* attitude, as I had just come from London. Alex and I couldn't even have a decent discussion, because when the younger students left the older students came over and sat up talking until three or four in the morning.

When Alex first arrived, I don't think he knew how to handle these young people. As a politician not often at home, he wasn't used to dealing with these matters. Besides, Alex was a real softie. In our home there had to be someone who wasn't soft, and that's where I came in. I believe one can only run an institution with discipline, as I did in my hospital ward and in my home. I tried to instil a degree of discipline at the mission in Cuba. You do as I say, I let the students know, or we ship you back home. But this was not well accepted. I was in a difficult position: to some degree I fell under Alex, not as his wife but as an ANC member. There could be only one captain on the ship – Alex – but when Alex was away, I was in charge.

On one occasion when Alex was travelling, I complained to Comrade Vernier, the Cuban Communist Party representative in charge of the ANC mission.

'This has got out of control,' I said. 'It's difficult to contact our ANC office in Zambia. Couldn't the Cuban authorities assist me in getting the students to stay at the boarding schools?'

Though it took a few months to sort things out with the Cubans' help, eventually I got the students out of our house. When Alex returned from his long trip he was quite pleased with my initiative. I think he was just happy to pass the buck to me.

This wasn't the end of our problems, though. Soon afterwards, Alex and I were told by Comrade Vernier that twelve ANC students at Nico Lopez School had been expelled for stealing food and liquor from the school kitchen. Trained dogs smelled the goods on them and led the Cuban authorities straight to where the ANC boys slept.

The guilty students were part of the first group sent from the military camps in Zambia by the MK leader Joe Modise.* They had the arrogant attitude that MK people were above all others. (This was true of some of the youngsters, but not of the chief of staff, generals or other leaders.) And these students were meant to be studying to become the future communist leaders of South Africa! After this incident, they were sent straight back to Zambia where the ANC rehabilitated them.

Alex and I agreed with the decision to expel the students. There was no excuse for their behaviour. Usually if the news wasn't for my ears I'd

---

* Johannes 'Joe' Modise (1929–2001) helped found Umkhonto we Sizwe (MK) following the Sharpeville Massacre in 1960. He received military training in the Soviet Union, Czechoslovakia and Vietnam. He was a key figure in winning acceptance of MK by several African governments, establishing MK bases in Tanzania, Angola and Uganda. As army commander in Angola, he suffered a mutiny by his troops in 1984. Modise served as South Africa's Minister of Defence from 1994 to 1999.

step aside, since Alex was head of the mission. But Comrade Vernier said, 'No, Blanche, I want you to listen to what is being said. You're the mother here.'

Much later we had a senior student, Thabo Mnisi, living with us. He'd studied medicine in Havana and qualified as a doctor. He was supposed to go back to South Africa but first he wanted to do a course in general surgery. He was told by Cuban authorities that he could pursue the surgery course on condition that he found his own accommodation. As there was a room and a shower for him in our house, Alex said he could stay. Thabo became almost like a son to us. Alex taught him what to do if one day he became a representative of the ANC. When both Alex and I travelled abroad, Thabo looked after the work of the mission.*

While things worked out well with Thabo, other students continued to have problems. We learned that the secondary school students had formed a union at school intended to unify students around the work of the ANC. What we didn't know was that the students disciplined each other by means of beatings. The students' union decided who was to be disciplined and who was not – a kangaroo court, more or less – and in one case they really injured a girl.

We were called to the school by Comrade Angel Delmau, who succeeded Comrade Vernier. He knew about the incident because the school principal had informed the Communist Party. In a communist country like Cuba, the Party runs everything, including the Education Department.

The principal didn't mince his words. He told us the students had caned the girl. 'Turn around and show your representative,' he said to her.

Across her upper thighs and lower bottom she had welt marks and was badly bruised.

'Didn't you protest?' we asked her.

'No,' she said. 'I felt it was the right thing because I was undisciplined.'

---

* Dr Thabo Mnisi, who died of cancer in 2006, was for many years clinical manager of the Alexandra Health Centre and University Clinic. Mnisi went into exile in 1977 and studied at the Higher Institute of Medicine in Santiago de Cuba, earning his medical degree and later returning to Havana to specialise in surgery.

We never found out what she had done. But that's what they were told: if you are undisciplined, you take your punishment. She could hardly sit! That's how I think her teachers discovered she needed treatment.

Alex and I spoke with the students. Then we informed ANC headquarters in Zambia about the incident through the diplomatic post, as we had done with previous disciplinary issues. A representative of the Cuban Communist Party later told Alex that they had expelled the girl leader and several boys who were in charge. We agreed with the decision and arranged for the ANC to have the students removed.

This beating was terrible, and in no way do I mean to excuse it. But we also understood that life in Cuba was difficult for the students. They had come to a different country and a different culture. They were far away from home and they fell back on what they knew. Some came from homes that didn't have proper discipline, where adults beat children, or perhaps the husband beat the wife. They learned violence not only in the home, but also in growing up under apartheid. I don't like to blame everything on apartheid, but apartheid caused a lot of damage, physically and psychologically.

The challenge for me and Alex was that we were in Cuba to do political work. We weren't told – or asked – to look after the students.

Blanche with Joe Nhlanhla, Alex and an interpreter, East Germany, 1972

The students didn't even know that our main work was political. Some of them assumed that they came first and that we were there just for them. It was the Cuban government that looked after them. But they had emotional needs, and that is where we came in. Though it wasn't easy, we did it because it had to be done.

○

Life in Cuba wasn't all work, though – far from it. Alex and I hosted some fabulous parties for our ANC students and their friends. The parties became so popular that on one occasion five hundred students filled the mission. It was a big house, but everyone had to squeeze in – they didn't care how!

The parties could only take place when Alex was home because he was the cook, and a good one at that. He'd make huge amounts of food in enormous pots that I'd brought over in a trunk from London. When one lot of students had eaten and another was just arriving, he'd cook another pot of paella or a big leg of ham. We fed everybody. We didn't want to turn people away. No, this was home and this was where our students would have their party.

We catered by saving extra food rations in the freezer, especially chicken and pork, and supplied the beer. While we treated the students like adults, they also had to know their limits. Alex said, 'Let them loose, knock their energies out. They're not going to misbehave.' We never had any problem with drunkenness or misbehaviour, largely because they appointed student marshals. The students would knock off their energies by dancing to a live Cuban band they'd hired. They'd rumba all through the night. I danced if they asked me to. I couldn't just stand apart from them – I even did the rumba! Though I took part, I made it clear that Alex and I were in control.

Eventually we had to discontinue the parties: they had got too big for the mission and became impossible for us to control. We were worried that things might get out of hand. But for as long as we held them, the parties were just great. I'll never forget the sight of Alex cooking up a big pot of stew with a smile on his face, welcoming everyone into the ANC mission.

Chapter 26

*'What I saw in the Soviet Union was the kind of life
I wanted to see in South Africa'*

Throughout our time in exile Alex played an important role in the
Afro-Asian Writers' Association (AAWA). Like other writers in
AAWA, Alex believed that poets and novelists should not just write
for art's sake but direct their art towards the cause of liberation for
oppressed peoples. The idea is that when you have a skill, you use it on
behalf of the oppressed. Like Alex, other writers in AAWA were leftist,
even Marxist, though the organisation itself wasn't specifically Marxist
because its focus was cultural.*

In 1969 Alex won the association's Lotus Prize for African and
Asian Literature. The award was presented to him in November 1970
in New Delhi by Indira Gandhi. Other Lotus Prize winners over the
years included Chinua Achebe from Nigeria, Ousmane Sembene from
Senegal, Ngugi wa Thiong'o from Kenya, and Agostino Neto, the first
president of post-colonial Angola.

From 1973 until the time of his death in 1985, Alex served as
secretary-general of the AAWA. In this capacity he worked closely with
Faiz Ahmed Faiz, the national poet of Pakistan and editor of *Lotus*
magazine, and Mu'in Tawfiq Bseiso, a brilliant Palestinian poet who was

---

* The Afro-Asian Writers' Association was formed by writers from 14 countries including the
USSR and China at a 1956 conference in New Delhi. The goal of the organisation was in part
to support the USSR 'as a bulwark of anti-imperialism, freedom … and socialism'. AAWA
writers generally subscribed to Marxism and to social realism in their writing. Many were
members of the Communist Party in their home countries.

deputy editor of *Lotus* and, like Alex, had won the Lotus Prize.*

The AAWA held conferences where poets and fiction writers could read their work and exchange ideas. These events included non-members. Among the South African exiles who travelled with us at one time or another were Ronnie Kasrils, Barry Feinberg and Barry Higgs. Writers first read their work in their own language and then it would be translated by an interpreter. Needless to say, this took a long time.

When we proposed toasts at the social functions after these events, I always expressed the hope that one day the South African people, especially students, would be able to read the work of our own poets in addition to the mainly English poets that we as students had had to study. Still today I hope that our government will encourage schools to read and study the work of South African poets, like Dennis Brutus and James Matthews, whose writing should not be forgotten.

In addition to his role in the AAWA, Alex was a longtime member of the World Peace Council (WPC), an organisation opposed to the proliferation of nuclear war. Romesh Chandra, WPC secretary-general, always chose Alex to accompany him to their conferences or asked him to act as his deputy if he had something more important to do.†

Alex's high position in these international organisations seemed to lead to jealousy in our own ranks. One time in London a friend nonchalantly remarked, 'So Alex was not an alcoholic?'

'Certainly not,' I said. 'Where does this come from?'

She wouldn't pursue the subject. Alex drank socially but always in moderation. And when life was hard he enjoyed a good drink. It gave him a chance to clear his mind. When he was tied down under house arrest, he took a good whisky or brandy or a glass of wine, but again in

---

* Faiz Ahmed Faiz (1911–84), a modern Urdu poet, was awarded the Lenin Peace Prize by the Soviet Union in 1962. Mu'in Tawfiq Bseiso (1926–84) was an Urdu poet who lived in Egypt. Each poet was imprisoned in his home country for several years because of his political activities.

† The World Peace Council, founded in 1949 and awarded official United Nations status, was later revealed as a front organisation of the Soviet Union. During the Cold War the WPC initiated demonstrations for nuclear disarmament and against United States involvement in Vietnam. Romesh Chandra, WPC general secretary and later president, was a member of the national committee of the Communist Party of India.

moderation, which is something in itself, given the enormous strain he was under. I can only put the woman's question about Alex's drinking down to jealousy, which rears its head even in liberation movements.

○

When Alex travelled to AAWA conferences and I accompanied him as his secretary, our hosts always wanted to show us a bit of their country. We went most frequently to Russia and the various republics of the Soviet Union. Writers who couldn't speak Russian – and most of them could not – were given a translator who spoke English. Sometimes I went to the interpreter's home and stayed over for the night.

The Soviet people could be so wonderfully ordinary. Whenever someone threw a party they'd say, 'Blanche, come round. We're going to have a party.' There was never that nose-in-the-air 'I'm a writer' attitude or 'I'm a big boy'. When we took a walk in a town we'd see the mayor walking along the street. The children and local people would go up and talk to her in a very ordinary fashion. A rare exception was the time in Uzbekistan when a man sitting next to me at a conference said, 'You know, *I'm* a minister' – meaning a cabinet member or parliamentary minister. 'Good for you!' I replied.

Many people in Russia read Alex's books in translation. He became a 'rouble millionaire'. I know because I saw the money coming in. It was with his roubles that he bought cameras for Eugene and Barto in Russia. Everywhere he went people wanted his autograph, even in central Asia. People came up to him because they recognised his face from the cover of his books. The Russians were great readers. In the underground trains everyone was reading a book. A leading professor in Russia said, 'Alex is read more in the Soviet Union than he is in South Africa.'

The Soviet Writers' Union paid my fare to its conferences and at one point even offered me a salary for assisting Alex as his secretary. I did a lot of work for him, typing his manuscripts and arranging his appointments. I always had paper and pen ready because whenever he was in Moscow writers and people from various organisations wanted to meet him. The Writers' Union tried to pay me because they believed in paying people who worked for them, and they considered me in this way because Alex was secretary-general of the Union. I turned down their offer. They had already paid my fare to Moscow, put me up in a hotel, and given me vouchers for food. They even gave me pocket money. I felt these benefits were more than enough compensation.

○

What I saw in the Soviet Union on our visits was the kind of life I wanted to see in South Africa. There was work for everybody and people worked reasonable hours. There was food for all and the food was cheap, so cheap in fact that people could eat at restaurants for just a few roubles. The people also enjoyed a high degree of culture. After work they'd come home in time to attend a performance of the opera or ballet for a small entrance fee.

Everyone had homes, or at least flats in complexes. Eugene's family lived with his mother-in-law in the same flat until they were moved into a flat of their own. I was told – though I never saw this – that in some places there was communal living with two or three families in a flat, but people were all housed. As I understood it, the crowding was temporary until families got their own flats. All I know is that there were no shacks. I never went into any area where the living conditions were nearly as harsh as in South Africa.

People might say, 'You saw it all through rose-coloured glasses.' I had the opportunity to talk not only with people in the hotels but also with ordinary people in the street as they went to the shops. Quite a few spoke English and everybody said they were happy. This is the impression they gave me. They might have expressed some dissatisfaction among themselves, but if they felt that way they wouldn't have been disloyal and declared it to anybody else.

In the important things of keeping body and soul together, communism succeeded. I have no hesitation at all in saying this, because it is what I worked for in South Africa, so that everybody might live together without want.

For Alex and me, going to Moscow was like Muslims going to Mecca. Seeing Lenin's tomb really touched me, because this was a man who brought together the philosophies of Marx, Engels and Lenin and made them a reality in the Soviet Union. Lenin symbolised all we stood for in international communism: work, housing, food and education for all. Beyond that, the Soviet Union gave great assistance to the peoples of Africa, Asia and Latin America ruled by fascist regimes.

Our connection to the Soviet Union was personal, too. Quite often we visited Eugene's family in Moscow. Once at the World Youth Festival in Moscow, we were told that we were being taken to meet an important person arriving at the airport. Looking over the heads of people at the arrivals hall, I saw a very tall young man with a wild mop of hair. 'There is my Barto!' I yelled. I had not seen him for such a long time that I was overcome with joy. I ran through everybody and jumped on him, wrapping my legs around him as he held onto me. The Soviets organised the Youth Festival not just to bring youth together, but to bring families together. They made it possible for Barto to visit all of us from East Germany.

○

When I look back on my life I'm struck by how much of the world I've been able to see, especially for a working-class girl from Cape Town like me. I've lived on three continents and in three quite different cultures, in Cape Town, London and Havana. Ironically, it was only when Alex and I left South Africa that we were able to see other parts of Africa for the first time as well: Angola, Mozambique and Zambia.

On an extensive trip just four months before Alex's death, we travelled to a festival in Moscow and then to Armenia and other republics before flying back to Moscow and Congo before returning to Cuba via London. Travelling so much was stressful on Alex, who'd had three heart attacks in the previous ten years. After we returned to Havana, he said, 'I'm not travelling again. I'm just going to stay here and write.' He had made his plans, and he was glad to be home.

Chapter 27

'Todo está bien, pero no más Alex'

One Friday in October 1985 I sat in the garden on a lovely afternoon writing letters to my mother, Eugene and Barto, and my brother in Canada. After a while I went inside to see what Alex was doing. He was cleaning his typewriter, which he'd received as a gift from someone in the Soviet Union.

He looked over at me and said, 'I'm going to write my autobiography. And I'm going to write a book about Cuba. And I'm going to write a novel about South Africa.'

Since his arrival in Cuba he had travelled so much to other countries that the only writing he did consisted of speeches. Now he had big plans as a writer. He had already started the novel. It was going to be about Umkhonto we Sizwe and the armed struggle and called *Crowns of Battle*.

I went back to my letter writing and he went to the bedroom to lie down. It was five o'clock in the afternoon.

When I looked in on him again, he was reading in bed. I liked to check on him just to have a small chat. I was always happy when he was home and we could talk. He was lying on his back – big, strong – holding his book. When I came back later he was asleep. I often checked his pulse while he slept. We had to be careful: he'd had three heart attacks previously. I never knew a heart that could tell you when it would attack. But that day he was sleeping so peacefully that I didn't check his pulse for fear of waking him. He was lying on his side, sleeping like a little baby. I thought, 'No, I don't want to disturb him.'

We were going to a reception that evening hosted by one of the embassies. After about an hour Alex woke and went to sit in his favourite armchair in the sitting room where he liked to relax. As I came in from the garden through the big french doors I passed by him and said, 'So, did you have a good sleep?'

'Yes.'

'What about a cup of tea then, darling?'

'Yes, but first get me a tablet. I've got heartburn.'

He was rubbing his chest vigorously.

'Pregnant women usually get heartburn, you know,' I said. 'I hope you're not pregnant!'

'Well, if I am, you're to blame.'

As I walked quickly to the bedroom to fetch a tablet from the medicine chest, I thought about the heart attacks he'd had before and the fact that he kept rubbing his chest. He'd stopped taking his special heart tablets after he'd finished the supply some months earlier, so I didn't have any in the cupboard.

When I gave him the antacid tablet he immediately began chewing rapidly, hungrily, almost wildly. Suddenly it dawned on me: Oh heavens, this isn't heartburn. This is a heart attack. He was chewing so aggressively that he was gasping and losing breath. His face was turning colour and he was rubbing his chest. It was painful. He knew he was having a heart attack.

I could not do CPR (cardio-pulmonary resuscitation) because he was sitting up in a chair. When you do CPR the person must be lying down so you can press on the heart, but I feared that if I put him on the floor he might die there. While he was in the chair, I tried but it didn't work.

'I'm wasting time,' I thought. 'Get the flying squad.'

I tried to call the ambulance but the phone didn't work, as sometimes happened. This was Cuba, the Third World.

I dashed next door and ran into Cariño, Cookie's sister, and told her Alex was having a heart attack. After summoning an ambulance, I ran back home with Inocencio hot on my heels. Alex had fetched his ECG reading from a previous heart attack. He was sitting on a dining-room chair, not saying anything. He gave me the cardiogram, hoping that if I caught the ambulance in time I could show them the results of the last graph. He'd turned significantly paler in colour. He didn't look frightened, but he was holding his chest, struggling to breathe. We had to get him to lie down.

'Inocencio, let's get Alex to the bedroom,' I said. I was in a state of terrible stress.

We tried to move Alex to the bed. But as we made our way I decided we couldn't wait for the ambulance and rushed to fetch the car. We placed Alex in the back seat. Inocencio sat next to him, holding him up. Alex had become even more ashen. He was losing oxygen. His breathing was heavy, laboured.

I turned on the lights, and pressed my foot on the pedal. We were off, heading for the nearest hospital. I drove madly with one hand, using the other to press the hooter. I passed through red lights, taking a quick look right and left before crossing over, and drove as fast as I could while trying to avoid an accident.

In Cape Town I'd learned to drive with my eyes on the rearview mirror to see if the Special Branch was following us. It was a habit I hadn't lost completely, and it helped me now. I had a clear view of Alex in the backseat. I could see his face turning ashen. I started weaving in and out of the traffic, driving with two wheels on the sidewalk to get around the slower cars. 'I must get there,' I thought. I was reckless, but I was on a desperate journey.

Just before the final turn to the hospital I got stuck on the narrow, two-lane airport road. It seemed all the odds were against me. The light was red. There were cars were in front and cars coming on the other side. It was rush hour. I could only sit and wait.

Then I heard Alex say, 'Blanche! Blanche!'

I looked back and saw his head fall onto his shoulder. I couldn't believe it; I refused to believe it.

In the meantime, the light changed to green and Inocencio jumped out of the car. Like a traffic policeman, he stopped the traffic to allow me to get ahead. I finally got through on the wrong side of the road and pulled up at the hospital.

A young doctor in green overalls was waiting for us with a stretcher at the entrance. I could only think that the ambulance must have phoned him, saying they'd gone to the house and found I had already left with Alex. With the help of Inocencio they lifted Alex onto the trolley and wheeled him into the hospital.

I stood outside with Inocencio. I imagine there were more doctors inside. The medical system was very good. They looked after their people well on the whole. I had also told them Alex was the representative for the ANC. They'd do all they could for anybody, but particularly for the representative of another country they were hosting.

I must have waited for an hour. Everything was quiet. Inocencio was trying to find a telephone to call Comrade Angel Delmau, the Communist Party member in charge of us. The telephone didn't work.

Eventually the surgeon came out, a slightly older man.

I said, 'El señor que está en' [the gentleman that's in there], 'mi esposo' [my husband]—'

He just looked at me. He didn't want to tell me. He tipped his head to the side and pointed to a woman doctor standing there, and then walked past me to wash his hands. She came over and took my hand in hers. 'Calma,' she said. 'Be calm.' I knew it was over.

'Calma. Su esposo ha fallecido.' (Your husband is dead.)

I still did not believe it.

'¿Mi esposo está muerto?' (Is my husband dead?)

My Spanish left me completely. I used the simple word for death.

'Sí, sí,' she said. 'Está muerto. Está muerto.' He's dead.

She told me that he had had a massive heart attack. They had tried to resuscitate him, to jolt his heart into action, but all their efforts failed.

I sort of died when she told me the news. I stood there like Lot's wife. I felt dead. Everything just collapsed.

She gave me a nudge and said, 'Señora. Señora.' And then she gave me Alex's shoe, which had fallen off. She also gave me his spectacles, which were broken. They had fallen off as they carried him in. This was all of him that was left.

I said to her in English, 'Take these back. I don't want them. Give him to me, but give him to me *alive*.'

Inocencio took me by the arm and said, 'Blanquita, vamos a su casa.' (I'm taking you home.)

It wasn't until I left the hospital that I realised fully that Alex had died. Then in hindsight it hit me: he didn't die at the hospital. He died in the car.

Inocencio and I got into the car and we drove home. When we stopped in front of our door, Inocencio said, 'Blanquita, esta es su casa.' (This is your house, Blanquita.)

'¿Cómo llegué? ¿Quién manejó el carro?' (But how did I get here? Who drove the car?)

'Blanquita, usted manejó el carro.' (You drove the car.)

'¿Yo? No entiendo.' (Me? I don't understand.)

I remember so many things from that day, but the journey home has never come back to me. I only know that I found myself in front of my house sitting behind the wheel of the car.

Cookie came out and asked, 'Blanquita. ¿Cómo está Alex?' (How's Alex?)

I remember shouting out, 'Cookie, es final! (It's final. It's over.) Todo está bien, pero no más Alex. No más.' (Everything is fine, but Alex is no more.)

I was so shocked I could not cry. Perhaps I couldn't allow myself to cry. Here I was, alone in Cuba after Alex's death. I had to stay firm and maintain the discipline. While I needed sympathy, I also needed to pretend I was in control of myself. I think that is why I said to Cookie, 'Todo esta bien, pero no mas Alex.' It was so *final*. Alex was gone for ever. But I also said, 'Everything is fine.' It was a forced control, which over the years I had learned to master.

Chapter 28

'He was my mentor, my lover, my everything'

I couldn't help wondering if I had done all I could to save Alex. Did I take the wrong route to the hospital? Did I do the right thing? Could I have done more? In the end I came to understand that I'd done my best. I did my best while he was alive, looking after him and loving him dearly. And I did my best at the time of his death. Everybody convinced me of that.

Cookie, Inocencio, Cariño and other neighbours came over to console me. The Swapo representative and his wife came, as did the Zimbabwe representative. At about eight o'clock on the day he died, comrades Vernier and Delmau of the Communist Party came to see me. I explained to them what had happened. They said, 'Blanche, he's had a heart condition. We know about it. We've got his medical history. We're not going to burden you with an autopsy.'

Comrade Vernier asked if I wanted to move out. They'd put me anywhere. They'd even accommodate me in a hotel where I could be among people, because I was alone. I declined.

I stayed in the house and waited for the boys to arrive from overseas for the funeral. Alex died on Friday, 11 October 1985, and the funeral was on 20 October, a Sunday. It had already been arranged that any member of the ANC who died in Cuba would be buried in Cuba – Alex, myself, anybody. We had no home but exile.

The Cuban authorities brought Eugene from Moscow and Barto from Zambia, paying all their expenses. When Barto arrived on Friday, one week after Alex's death, Comrade Delmau said, 'Blanche, the family's here. Let me know if you first want to get together and think about anything.' The Cubans all did so much for us. I remember Delmau saying, '*Anything*, Blanche. Just say what you need. Whatever you want, we'll do for you.'

The organisations that supported us throughout our stay in Cuba came forward to assist me in this difficult time. They were all, of course, Communist Party members working under the central committee. They looked after us as if we were their own. After everything was over, I wrote a letter to the central committee, thanking them for all they had done.

The central committee brought a book of condolences to the house, and the Minister of Foreign Affairs was the first to sign it, along with ambassadors of countries and representatives of other liberation organisations. The Cuban public lined up to sign the book, with the queue sometimes stretching outside our door. When the news of Alex's death made its way to Moscow and South Africa and all over the world, messages of condolence came flooding in, so much so that I had to open a special box at the post office to receive all the mail.

The authorities also arranged for a photo of Alex to be enlarged and put against the wall. They made sure I had enough food in the house for the people who came in to pay their respects, including the ANC students, some of whom seemed permanently hungry. The Cubans supplied me with extra coffee, too, because Cuban hospitality requires that you offer your guests coffee, and Cubans drink a lot of it. Without exception, the Cubans gave me support, not only financial but moral support. Nobody could have done more.

I thought, 'Too bad Alex isn't here.' It was a stupid thought, but one is only human. One thinks those things. I'd rather have done without all the care and attention and have Alex back with me. If only he could be there – alive, in the house, chatting over a cup of tea – then all these things would not have been necessary.

The Cubans put Eugene and Barto up in a hotel – not just any hotel, but one of the big, beautiful, posh hotels on the waterfront. They were given rooms that cost a pretty penny. The Cubans told them they could order as much food and drink as they wanted. They were celebrating Alex's life, after all. All Eugene had to do was sign for anything they ordered. Of course, all of the boys' 'pals' came over – ANC students, Cuban students and others who knew Alex but had never actually met Eugene and Barto.

When Delmau came to see if they were happy, he looked at the bill and said, 'What's going on? Look at this bill! You're not eating. You're not drinking. Why aren't you celebrating Alex's life? Alex had a very rich life. Drink on it. Have a good time and get this whole thing of your father's death out of your system.' It was then that the boys and their friends went to town.

The next morning, when we went to see the body before it was entombed, was difficult for all of us. Alex was lying in state in a large open hall at the cemetery. Several hundred people passed by to pay their respects. But before the body was taken to the main hall for public viewing, Eugene and Barto saw Alex's body in a private room. It affected them badly, but it was probably as well that it did. I couldn't let go like that. I wish I could have broken down the way they did.

Alex had been embalmed and kept in the mortuary for a week. It was summer and hot. His face seemed like a mask. And that mask, that final drawing in of his chin, seemed to indicate the terrible pain of his last moments. I could tell that the pain must have wrenched him. When Alex was in a London hospital recuperating from a previous heart attack, he wrote a little story about a man in his ward who died. He described the muscles pulling hard, tearing away from the heart. Looking at Alex lying there, I thought that this is what must have happened to him. I should never have seen him that way. I should have just remembered him as he was when alive. That image stayed with me for a time.

The funeral began at three o'clock precisely. Alfred Nzo, the secretary-general of the ANC, who had come from Zambia, gave the oration.* He was the only ANC official there, though many others

---

* Alfred Nzo (1925–2000) was an ANC activist from Alexandra township who served in exile as ANC foreign representative in Cairo, India, Zambia and Tanzania. He was elected secretary-general of the ANC in 1969 and re-elected in 1985. In 1994 he was named by Nelson Mandela as Minister of Foreign Affairs.

sent letters and telegrams from all over the world – London, Moscow, Lusaka, and elsewhere. Nzo read an account of all that Alex had done for the Movement, beginning with his role in Cape Town and the Treason Trial. An interpreter translated into Spanish. I don't remember all of it. I was still trying to recover from the shock. They lifted the coffin up onto the car and took Alex to be entombed.

Alex was buried in the same large plot where the mother of José Martí lies.* Cuban cemeteries have beautiful tombs, some with statues rising above them, which people come to see. José Martí was a national hero, almost the Lenin of Latin America, and so his mother is also a hero.

Two years later, after I had moved back to London, the Cuban authorities wanted me to return to observe the remains of Alex being exhumed. Because of a shortage of burial space, they remove the body after two years to make room for another. The coffin is lifted out and the body reburied in a graveyard somewhere else. By then they don't need such a big space, only a small hole, because they repack the remains neatly in a small concrete case.

A team of ANC people came to see me about this in London, including Frene Ginwala.† She brought a letter from Delmau asking me to come for the exhumation, which she'd received while with a team of ANC people visiting Cuba. I wrote to Delmau saying that it would be re-living Alex's death and burial if I were to come back and see the exhumation. If some member of the family had to be there, couldn't they ask Eugene, or perhaps Eugene and Barto? I think they wanted me to come but I eventually ignored the request. I could never go back and live through it all again.

I didn't want to see Alex's body exhumed because I'd already seen an exhumation once and that was enough. A few years earlier, one of our adult ANC students had suddenly died. Some time after, the Cuban

---

* José Julián Martí Pérez (1853–1895) was a poet, essayist, journalist, professor, publisher and political theorist. Through his writings and political activity, he became a symbol for Cuba's bid for independence against Spain in the 19th century. He is known as the 'Apostle of Cuban Independence.'

† Frene Noshir Ginwala (born 1932) was Speaker of the National Assembly of South Africa from 1994 to 2004. Before and during her exile, she worked in Tanzania, Zambia, Mozambique and the United Kingdom as an ANC official, a journalist and a broadcaster.

authorities asked Alex to observe the student's exhumation as the ANC representative. I went along. It was a new experience for both of us.

Two men with gloves lifted the box out of the tomb and emptied the remains. The body hadn't fully disintegrated. The skeleton was still intact, bones with no skin. Then they took the body apart piece by piece, twisting and tearing the bones until they detached, one by one. Just a twist and most bones came right off. It was all done within seconds.

I don't know why but I started laughing and crying at the same time. I almost went hysterical. They chopped the body up so that the pile of bones fitted into a little concrete box about half a metre square. They put the head on top. By that time I had almost completely lost it. 'Tell the head it's getting shorter!' I thought. I couldn't stop laughing. Alex said to me, 'Just go and stand over there. You shouldn't have come here at all.'

That is why when they asked me to see Alex exhumed, I thought I would never want to see my husband being torn apart. I had no intention of going. He could stay where he was. After all, we had made a pact that if one of us died, in whatever country we were in, we'd be buried there and that would be it. That is where we'd stay. What was the point of going to visit the grave? It wasn't necessary. After death there is nothing more.

$$\circlearrowleft$$

I think about Alex a lot: the funny things he said, the serious things, his words of advice about politics and life in the Struggle. Alex was often referred to as an intellectual, his wife not at all. But he never treated me as if I wasn't. He was always so patient and understanding. Though he was not demonstrative, he must have loved me inwardly.

It's strange. I did most of the work at home. Yet when Alex wasn't there, I felt I didn't know what to do. He was a shoulder to lean on. He was my mentor, my lover, my everything.

People asked him, 'How do you keep on with this work? What makes you tick? Why do you keep on and on?' He would reply, 'You must have a spirit of adventure, a sense of humour, and a little knowledge of history. That keeps you going.' And that's how Alex carried on.

Sometimes when I look at the political situation today I think, 'Good heavens. What would Alex say?' He once said to me, 'You know, when we go back, I'll go and sit on the hill – Table Mountain is a bit high, but I'll sit on Signal Hill – and I'll watch all of them scrambling for positions in Parliament.' That's exactly what happened. I can see Alex as if he were alive, sitting and looking down on Parliament from Signal Hill.

Alex being congratulated by his son Eugene and Blanche on a Soviet award in Moscow

Chapter 29

'The best part of our exile was spent in Cuba'

In the weeks after Alex's death I had terrible headaches, painful tension headaches across the right eye back to the middle of the head on the right side. The pain was so bad I was awake for much of the night. I drank one Disprin right after the other.

Fortunately, the Cuban people were there to support me. My immediate neighbours, the surrounding neighbours, members of ICAP and OSPAAAL, the man who was in charge of us – Delmau – they were around me all the time. I didn't have a chance to feel sorry for myself. But it was difficult all the same. I was by myself in a strange country. I knew I had to keep firm, that I mustn't collapse. I thought back to the time when I came out of detention and didn't allow myself to cry. Then I had to remain strong for Eugene and Barto; now it was for myself.

I stayed on in Cuba for the time being only because Alf Nzo asked me to. Immediately after the burial I already started packing because I knew I was going to leave. Then Nzo asked me to stay on as the ANC representative. But I just couldn't. I was too emotionally upset, still trying to recover from the shock. Nzo's request seemed ridiculous. I felt it was insensitive even to ask. Alex had just died. It wasn't that he'd been ill and I had been nursing him. He died *suddenly*. And now I was expected to act as if nothing had happened.

In addition, without Alex I couldn't do the work. It's amazing. Even in Cape Town, if he was under house arrest he'd be in the house writing and I could do all that needed to be done. But when he was detained it was much more difficult for me because he just wasn't there. His presence had a powerful effect on me.

I asked Nzo that I be relieved of the post in Havana.

'Since I can't go to South Africa, I want to leave Cuba and go back to London. I've got a home in London. I've got a job—'

'What work will you do?' Nzo asked.

'I'll either work for *Soviet Weekly* or maybe Defence and Aid.'

Nzo then said that the ANC often took a long time to find a replacement for a post. Would I be prepared to stay on until they did?

'Well, as long as it doesn't take too long,' I said.

I didn't want to stay in Cuba. But I did because I was asked. I couldn't walk out. It was a job that had to be done. But inside I was broken, torn apart, and I really couldn't cope.

Nzo wasn't the only one who wanted me to stay. Thabo Mnisi, the young man who lived with us, also tried to persuade me. He was very disappointed when later I left.

In the meantime Eugene told me the Soviet Writers' Union had said that if I wanted to come to Moscow and live there, they would give me a flat. Alex had been a leading figure in the Writers' Union and they wanted to take care of me. But if they were paying for me, it meant they were keeping me. I was only fifty-eight and I wasn't going to be kept by anyone.

'I'm not going to be a kept woman,' I told Eugene.

In November, a month after Alex's death, my lawyer in London, Henry Brown, wrote to inform me that the estate should be wound up. As I was chief executor, Henry said it would help if I went to London to see to the will, our house and the finances, and to sign various papers. So in December I travelled to London to attend to these affairs, even though it was difficult to make arrangements during the Christmas holiday. At one point I said to Henry in London, 'I must get away from Alex. I must get back to London for good.'

Henry advised me: 'Blanche, write a letter to the ANC giving the date when you want to be back in London.' And so I wrote to ANC headquarters in Lusaka, informing them of my wishes.

On 8 January 1986 I returned to Havana to speak on the anniversary of the founding of the ANC. I was still in Havana two months later on 21 March, when I spoke at the commemoration of the 1960 Sharpeville Massacre. It had now been five months since Alex's death, and the ANC still hadn't sorted out my future. It was an unnecessary delay. I was told only that the ANC had not yet given permission to the Cuban authorities to allow me to leave. I thought, 'I'm not a puppet on a string. I'm a human being. I should be allowed to go.' But in fact I could go only when the ANC said I could. What nonsense!

It was only with the help of O.R. Tambo that I was finally allowed to leave Cuba in April 1986.* O.R. occasionally came to Cuba to attend a conference or to speak with Fidel Castro about co-operation between Cuba and the ANC. Alex used to write reports for O.R. to assist with these discussions, though he didn't attend the meetings. According to the ANC students, O.R. told them that in Alex they had one of the best minds in the ANC and that they should exploit his expertise – which they did.

We visited O.R. whenever he came to Cuba. I'd got to know him in London, though he was more often in Lusaka. His wife Adelaide lived not far from us in Muswell Hill. All of us in the ANC looked up to O.R., almost as a father figure. He'd see me walking along the road carrying parcels, stop the car and send his son over to assist with the bags and take me home.

I once asked him, 'O.R., when are we going home?'

'Blanche, be patient,' he said. 'It's going to be a long, protracted struggle.'

'But when does the protraction come to an end? I want to go home!'

'It's a long struggle, Blanche. Just keep on with the good work.'

After Alex's funeral, when I told Alf Nzo that I couldn't continue in Cuba, O.R. sent me a nice letter in which he said he understood and respected what I felt, and that I would soon be relieved of my position.

---

* O.R. Tambo (1917–1993) was president of the ANC in exile from 1967. Along with Nelson Mandela, his legal partner in Johannesburg, and Walter Sisulu, he was a founding member of the ANC Youth League in 1944. After the 1960 Sharpeville massacre, Tambo was sent overseas by the ANC to set up the ANC's international mission and mobilise international opinion against apartheid.

He said he had given instructions to that effect.

Now in March 1986, O.R. was in Cuba to see Fidel.* I had been told by Angel Delmau that we could greet him at the Havana airport. His entourage had arrived ahead of him – Gertrude Shope, who was in charge, one or two other women, and three or four men.

When O.R. arrived, he greeted his entourage first while I held back. Then he saw me and asked, 'Blanche, what are you doing here?'

'Yes, Comrade O.R., I'm still here.'

We didn't discuss it then, but I'd been having problems getting my departure documents – my ticket and so forth – because the ANC hadn't carried out O.R.'s instructions. The Cubans who were in charge of me hadn't received word from the ANC that I could go.

That night, while O.R. was still sitting in the VIP lounge at the airport, the Cuban authorities handed me my ticket to London. They must have known that O.R. would ask for this, because they had the ticket ready.

Later he called me. I went to see him in the house where he was staying.

'Blanche, I'm very angry because I had your request to leave and I gave instructions that you should be going,' he said. 'This was a while ago. I can't understand why they ignored my instructions.' He had in fact given permission for me to leave as early as Alex's funeral. Someone had held on to this information and meanwhile I was falling apart. After I received my ticket, I packed my bags and returned to London, as I had tied up everything long before then.

◯

The best part of our exile was spent in Cuba. Our life there was good. We'd work for a while, and the rest of the day we had free to sit and contemplate or go out. Quite often I went to the boulevard that runs all along the beach in Havana Street. I would sit and look at the sea. It reminded me of Cape Town and made me feel good.

---

* During O.R. Tambo's visit to Cuba in 1986, Fidel Castro surprised the ANC delegation by pointing out the practical, economic need for compromise in a negotiated settlement with the apartheid regime.

Alex and I had no other comrades, so we had more time to enjoy each other's company. I'd sit in the garden and write letters to friends and family. He'd write a general letter for everybody so that we kept in touch with all our family and friends.

Cuba was more comfortable than London, which is a big city that could eventually become a bit boring. We didn't go for all that London had to offer, once we had seen all the sights. In the Struggle we were occupied with political work all the time. Occasionally we had a party with friends, but basically it was political work. In addition, we had so little money or time to enjoy London.

Cuba was a good example, not only for Alex and me, but for all of us who went into exile, of how a people working together can rebuild their country. Cuba had won what we were hoping to win and we were able to learn how they had gone about it. Batista had crippled Cuba.* The industries had not been built up. Cuba was still mainly an agricultural country, struggling to survive. With the rebirth of their country under the powerful icon and strong character of Fidel Castro, Cubans would say, 'Viva Fidel, viva Cuba!' And I would add my own, 'Viva Fidel! Viva Cuba!'

Though life in Cuba wasn't perfect, Cuba meant a lot to Alex and me. It was home. When we were abroad – in Moscow, for example – we'd say, 'Well, it's time to go home now.' But where was home? Where were we going? South Africa? London? No, we were going to Cuba. We were going home. The Cubans sing a song, *Cuba qua Linda es Cuba* (Cuba, Beautiful Cuba.) That's a song we also sang.

○

Alex's death continued to haunt me. In April 1986 I flew from Cuba via Berlin back to London. I was met by Denis Goldberg and my friend Nancy Dick. I'd lost so much weight that Nancy did not recognise me. I stayed with her until I moved back into the house I shared with Hettie September.

---

* Fulgencio Batista y Zaldívar (1901–73) was leader and dictator of Cuba from 1933 to 1944 and from 1952 to 1959, before being overthrown in the Cuban Revolution.

The *Soviet Weekly* offered me a job to work as a photo librarian, organising pictures that had been processed in Moscow. We also had transparencies of almost everything in the Soviet Union, including marvellous paintings that could be reprinted in books for a small fee. This was all part of the larger work of providing information about the Soviet Union to Western publishers and the press during the Cold War.

Though I was constantly busy, I enjoyed the work. The phone rang non-stop. I went in early to get my work done, leaving home around seven on a sixteen-station train journey so I could start at eight instead of nine. But I didn't find this a burden. As a nurse in South Africa and England and an activist in the Movement, I worked under an almost military discipline. Work at *Soviet Weekly* was among my least stressful jobs.

About this time I was also offered a position in the ANC at headquarters in Lusaka, Zambia. I turned it down, because while I was in Havana I'd heard from one of the ANC women attending school in Cuba what was happening in Lusaka, and I wasn't going to take a chance. She was a coloured woman, perhaps in her late forties, studying at a tertiary school for women while her three sons studied at the secondary school. After fleeing South Africa in the wake of the 1976 Soweto Uprising, she had first worked for the ANC in Zambia before coming to Cuba. She told me that the women in Lusaka were being harassed – in fact, raped.* Other people who had been there confirmed what she said.

I turned down the position because I felt that if she was telling the truth, the same thing could happen to me, and I'd have no safeguard. Alex wouldn't be there and others could just say, 'We don't know about it.' It's like the young woman who brought a charge of rape against Jacob Zuma. They demeaned her and made as if it didn't really happen.†*

---

* Women in the ANC and MK camps faced multiple forms of discrimination and abuse, including sexual harassment, sexual abuse including rape and unwanted pregnancies. These problems were exacerbated by the huge disparity between the number of male and female comrades.

† Jacob Zuma, President of South Africa and the ANC, was charged with rape in the Johannesburg High Court. The accuser, a 31-year-old family friend, was a member of a prominent ANC family and an AIDS activist. On 8 May 2006, the court dismissed the charges, agreeing with Zuma that the sexual act in question was consensual.

I didn't know if the ANC was aware of the 'harassment', or if they didn't want to know. I just did what I thought was good for me. In order to safeguard my dignity, my soul and myself, I decided not to go.

Not taking the job offer didn't sit well with a lot of people. When a high-ranking member of the ANC executive in London asked me why I'd turned down the offer, I admitted, 'This is indiscipline.' When the Movement gives you a task, you don't turn it down – they need you to fulfil that task. But I wouldn't go under just any circumstances. And that is why I said no. Alex would have agreed with me. And even if he hadn't, I would rather have lost my position in the ANC than have my soul destroyed.

Chapter 30

'I was never given the chance to say goodbye'

When President F.W. de Klerk announced the release of Nelson Mandela and the unbanning of the ANC and SACP in February 1990, it was a joyous occasion in London. Trafalgar Square exploded in jubilation. Many South Africans were there, exiles and non-exiles, members of the Anti-Apartheid Movement and non-members. The British public rejoiced with us, as did other foreigners in the UK fighting for their countries to be liberated too. Though it was a cold and bleak February day, it felt warm and as if the sun shone. Some of my fellow South Africans immediately went to their houses to start packing in the hope of going home.

SACP members in London met at a member's house to commemorate the end of the Party's clandestine work. I wasn't invited to the celebration – I was not even told about it. When I phoned some of my fellow members, wanting to wish them well, I couldn't get hold of any of them. I went to the house of one and found the curtains drawn. I knocked and somebody slightly opened the curtain but quickly closed it. I went home. The strange circumstances made me think something had happened, but I didn't know what it could have been. Later, when one of the Party members asked why she hadn't seen me at the gathering, I told her I hadn't been invited. She didn't say where the celebration was held, and I didn't ask.

In view of the otracism, I assumed I'd been expelled from the Party, though I was never told. From that point on I was not asked to fulfil any more Party tasks, nor was I informed of Party activities. I had been a loyal Party member, had belonged to a Party cell and had fulfilled any tasks given to me by the central committee. When I returned to South Africa in 1995, I applied to receive the Party magazine, *The African Communist*, but did not get a reply.

I can only guess at the motives behind these doings. Perhaps it was because Alex and I had defied Party leaders by not stopping Eugene's marriage to Lena. I also refused to stay in Cuba and then declined to go to Zambia. These were considered acts of indiscipline. Perhaps some members were also jealous of the international recognition Alex had received for his literary and political work. None of this was spelled out, of course. Similar matters happen in many political parties, and if I allowed these events to upset me I'd be miserable most of the time. The pain of Alex's death was much worse than being ostracised from the Party, so I didn't let any of this affect me.

○

Throughout the years I'd kept in touch with my mother. Whenever I got extra money – a bonus, for example – I'd send it home to help her out. With additional support from my brother George in Canada, she was able to live quite well in Cape Town in her later years.

In late 1989 she became ill with a heart condition. My niece Carol, who was taking care of her, told me my mother was dying. I wanted to see her before she closed her eyes for the last time, but I wasn't allowed home: the South African security police denied me that opportunity. I had left the country on an exit permit and thus was no longer considered a South African citizen. I couldn't return unless I had a visa. Several times I applied for a visa, and each time my application was rejected. I then applied to Pretoria on compassionate grounds.

I was eventually given the visa in part because I wrote in my application that I wanted to visit my aged mother, other members of the family, relatives and friends, *and* see the great beauty of Cape Town and South Africa. My lawyer Himie Bernadt explained to me that if I had only asked to see my mother, they would have said, 'Your mother's dead. You can't come.'

But even before South Africa approved my visa, the security police and officials from the Home Affairs office in Cape Town actually visited my mother to see whether I was telling the truth about her illness. Carol called to tell me that plainclothes men had come right into my mother's room to have a look. They found her lying there, what little was left of her, 96 years old and dying. What an indignity! She died shortly afterwards on 3 December 1990.

Three weeks after my mother's death I was finally given permission to come home. On the flight into Cape Town a young white woman next to me hugged me and broke into tears, saying, 'I haven't seen Table Mountain for three years!' I, too, began to cry and said, 'I have not seen Table Mountain for more than twenty.'

I remembered how in the days before our departure in 1966 I had cried bitterly whenever I looked at Table Mountain, how Alex had tried to comfort me by saying, 'Never mind. We'll work our way back, and we will return one day. You will see Table Mountain again.' Now I saw the mountain, but not in the circumstances I desired.

I did come back, though, to a tearful welcome at Cape Town airport from my family and friends. My own tears were a mixture of sadness for not having Alex, Eugene and Barto with me, and joy for the warm welcome I received.

Even at this late date, my visa came with a banning order. I had to stay with Carol at the address I gave and not move from there until my departure. I couldn't attend any university or school or place of learning. I couldn't go to a factory. I couldn't have any interviews. When the *Cape Argus* called for an interview, I had to turn them down. Himie had told me, 'Look, you'd better carry out what they say, as we have not yet taken over and negotiations are still on with the Nats. They might detain you if you don't adhere to their instructions.'

I also had to be out of the country by 21 March. Home Affairs and the Wynberg security police phoned once a week, every week, to remind me that I was still under a banning order. I was so excited to be home that I forgot why 21 March was such an important date. It was only on the plane going back to London that it occurred to me that 21 March is

Human Rights Day, the day in 1960 on which 69 unarmed people were shot and killed during a peaceful demonstration at Sharpeville to oppose the pass system. That was why I had to be out of the country.

I was a 62-year-old woman who wanted to visit her dying mother, but I was still a security threat. By the time I arrived my mother had died. I also missed her funeral and burial. I was never given a chance to say goodbye. I did not see the last bit of her breath, the rising and falling of her breast and the heart within still beating. I have never lived that down.

○

With the collapse of the Soviet Union in 1991, *Soviet Weekly* closed. I received a generous payout. I had never had so much money before. For our entire adult life I had little money. To manage our meagre finances I'd lock myself in the bedroom while Alex took Eugene and Barto out of the house and I'd stretch that threepence into sixpence without robbing anybody and yet managing to pay everybody. Alex would never spend anything on himself, even when he needed shoe repairs, so I bought his

The staff of Soviet Weekly, *1991*

things, some of which were quite expensive. But I didn't mind, because when he was under house arrest I thought, 'He's giving up so much. Let him at least look and feel nice when he's walking about. Let him feel a degree of dignity.'

Now I had money every month to live on. After I lost my job at *Soviet Weekly*, I took another job as supervisor of a cleaning firm in London for a year or two, overseeing the work of three or four cleaners in a primary school every afternoon. I did the work just to buy extras and pay the petrol for my car, which I used to scoot around London. After about a year or two at the cleaning firm, I decided I had had enough. I could now live on what I had.

○

On the day of South Africa's first fully democratic election, 27 April 1994, everybody was so keen to vote. Long queues wound around the South African Embassy, previously a symbol of apartheid where I and so many other comrades now went to exercise our democratic right. The queues were equally long at voting stations throughout London. It was tremendous. We felt so proud to vote for Mandela and the ANC. While we were waiting to go in, we gathered in little groups in the queue and chatted. Afterwards we went to the pub and toasted the occasion over drinks, preparing to live in our new freedom. We were joined by many of our British anti-apartheid friends. What we'd worked so hard for had now come about. London was electric with feeling.

I thought about Alex, how in fact he wouldn't have enjoyed being in London to vote because he would have wanted to go home.

○

For all of us who left the country on exit permits in the 1960s, the election changed everything. We were now considered South African citizens and eligible to receive passports and come home. Many South Africans I knew in London had already left to help negotiate the peaceful transition to a new government. Apparently I was wanted too. A few years ago I spoke with Amina Cachalia at a women's meeting at the Mount Nelson Hotel in Cape Town.* She said, 'Blanche, you know at Madiba's inauguration he called a committee and said, "Get Blanche. Blanche La Guma must be here." And Blanche La Guma was sitting in England.'

When I received official notification of my change in status, I dropped my hands to the table, sighed, and thought to myself, 'I'm going home.'

I told Henry Brown, who'd become almost like a guardian to me, of my wish to return to South Africa. 'Blanche, think very carefully,' he said. 'You've been away for nearly thirty years, and you'll have to find out whether you can really make it there. Changes have taken place. Can you really go and live there? It's so different. You are now used to living here in this kind of environment. Find out. Go over and take a holiday. We'll see to the finances.'

So I came to Cape Town on a holiday, this time without a banning order. I again stayed with Carol. Before long I knew I was home. After just a few weeks I phoned Henry. 'I'm staying,' I said. 'I'm not coming back.'

'Blanche! You've got some loose ends to tie up here,' Henry said.

Henry was right. We were also told by the ANC, 'Don't come home if you don't have a job and a home to come to.' The ANC obviously couldn't support everybody, and I had neither a home nor a job. So I didn't rush to get home until I had sorted things out properly in London. When I found I could make it financially in South Africa without a job and that I could stay with Carol, I decided to come home. I was making another move, the last of the moves that had taken me from Cape Town to London to Havana and now home again.

○

It was over for me in exile. I'd done my job and I'd succeeded. My first job, to fight and get rid of apartheid, was done. 'I've done my share,' I told myself. 'I'll have to get settled soon in Cape Town.'

---

*   Amina Cachalia (born 1930) is a veteran anti-apartheid and women's rights activist. She was a founding member of the Federation of South African Women (Fedsaw) in 1954, serving as its treasurer.

I was among the last to leave South Africa in 1966 with Alex, Eugene and Barto. Now I was among the last to return in 1994. Even as I returned I felt sad, because when we left we had left as a family of four, but now I was returning alone. Eugene was already in Cape Town, having moved from Moscow with his wife and family in 1992. Barto was married and working in Berlin. I was returning alone. It was heart-wrenching to come back to Cape Town without Alex.

Chapter 31

'The next generation must now take on the work'

I returned home on 19 June 1994 in the middle of a wet Cape Town winter, one month after Nelson Mandela's inauguration in Pretoria. I was struck by some of the physical changes I saw, for example road changes and additions. Yet some of the beaches and scenic places I was shown by friends were just as they had been all those years while we were here.

My friend Dolly Wiid took me on a trip up the coast.

'Good heavens, Dolly!' I said. 'We have taken over in government for just this short while and look at all the improvements that have been made.'

'No, Blanche,' she said. 'This was here all the time, but you couldn't come here and neither could I. We were barred from seeing it.'

The saddest part for me was that communities that had existed in earlier years had broken up. The friendliness had disappeared. People didn't want to mix as they had in earlier years. Everyone kept to himself. It was sad but understandable, because of the forced removals under the Group Areas Act. Families were separated, married children moved away from their parents, and longstanding friends and neighbours were separated and had to fit into new environments. Children also had to make new friends. The biggest heartbreak of all was the bulldozing of District Six, the heart-throb of Cape Town, a vibrant mixture of mainly coloured families, the place where Alex was born and bred.

The ANC had also changed. I went to the ANC branch in Claremont and offered to help in any way I could.

'Give me anything to do,' I said to the lady sitting there. 'I'll lick stamps. I'll stuff envelopes. The kitchen looks a bit awkward. Can I clean the —?'

'Oh, no. Don't do that. There's nothing to do.'

'There *can't* be nothing to do,' I said. 'There must be something. I worked in the Movement for many, many years.'

She didn't understand what work could be done in a liberation movement. But it was no longer a liberation movement. It had now become a government. It was quite clear she was just doing a job. In the past we never just did a job. We never even got paid for the work we did. We were committed to something larger.

Eventually she said I could stuff envelopes. While we were working, she told me there was going to be an ANC meeting.

'How many at a meeting? How many belong to the ANC?' I asked.

She said there were sixty ANC members in Claremont.

'Great!' I said. 'Never had that many before.'

I went and we were about fourteen, no different from the earlier days when our meetings were banned. It seems once the ANC government was in place, people were content to leave the running of things to those in Parliament. They had ceded their rights to them. They didn't realise they had to go to meetings and have their say. I found a friend there and said to him, 'Man, we're back to square one.' An election was coming up but people weren't saying anything. I thought, I'm out of this. I'm finished now.

I realised then that the first phase was over: we had won the battle against apartheid. The next generation must now take over the work. Times had changed, and methods of operating had altered. It was difficult for me to fit in with this new lot. I still came with the old hardliner attitude. I saw people being too lax, with a sort of easy-going nonchalance. The old ANC would have kept everything in tip-top shape, because that showed part of your character, which would carry over into your other work. The kitchen was full of dirty cups. 'I'll wash those cups,' I said. 'No, you mustn't wash the cups. Somebody else is coming to do that.' But it was not being done. Discipline was required, and that is what I found lacking.

My final work for the ANC involved canvassing for a council election about a year after I returned. I did it the old style, going from house to house. I went to help Fred Carneson in a rather depressed area in Plumstead. The lifts were out of order at some of the flats, so I had to take the stairs. At one place I fell down the stairs and injured my leg and my ankle.

When Barto phoned that night, I told him I was nursing a bad ankle from my fall.

'What the heck are you still canvassing for?' he shouted at me. 'Don't you know that others must now take over? You've done your share. Where are the young people? Why aren't they canvassing?'

I thought, 'He's correct. I fought apartheid with every bone of my body: I was angry, and I wanted to see it come right. Now, finally, it had. It was time that I stop.'

Now I do as I please because I'm finished with all the discipline and regimentation of the Movement and the Communist Party. I spend my days reading the newspapers, meeting with friends, window-shopping, and taking walks along Main Road. Some of what I lived through was terribly traumatic, leaving a deep-seated wound that's taken a long time to heal. Writing this book has given me the chance to get all that pain out of my system.

Bibliography

The editor is indebted to the following sources for information included in the footnotes.

For the history of Cape Town, including the First and Second World Wars, cultural organisations, the development of apartheid, and political resistance: *Cape Town in the Twentieth Century: An Illustrated Social History* by Vivian Bickford-Smith, Elizabeth van Heyningen and Nigel Worden (Cape Town, David Philip, 1999). Also helpful was André Odendaal and Roger Field's 'Introduction' to *Liberation Chabalala: The World of Alex La Guma* (Bellville: Mayibuye Books, 1993).

For the history and culture of the coloured community in Cape Town: M. Adhikari, *Not White Enough, Not Black Enough: Racial Identity in the South African Coloured Community* (Athens, Ohio: Ohio University Press and Cape Town: Double Storey Books, 2005); Leopold Bloom, 'The Coloured People of South Africa', *Phylon* 28, 2 (1967), 139–150; Keith Buchanan and N. Hurwitz, 'The "Coloured" Community in the Union of South Africa', *Geographical Review* 40, 3 (July 1950), 397–414; Abe Desmore, 'The Cape Coloured People To-Day: An Address Delivered to the League of Coloured Peoples, London', *Journal of the Royal African Society* 36, 144 (1937), 347–356; Grant Farred, *Midfielder's Moment: Coloured Literature and Culture in Contemporary South Africa* (Boulder, Colorado: Westview Press, 2000); Hermann Giliomee, 'The Non-Racial Franchise and Afrikaner and Coloured Identities, 1910–1994', *African Affairs* 94, 375 (April 1995), 199–225; and J. Gunther Stuhardt and Sydney V. le Grange, 'Coloured Folk of South Africa', *Phylon* 1, 3 (1940), 203–213.

For the war years Louis Grundlingh's essays were especially helpful: 'The Role of Black South African Soldiers during the Second World War: A Contested Contribution', *Historia* 44, 2 (1999), 345–364; and 'Prejudices, Promises, and Poverty: The Experiences of Discharged and Demobilized Black South African Soldiers after the Second World War', *South African Historical Journal* 26 (1992), 116–135.

For histories of political resistance in the twentieth century: Jack Simons and Ray Simons, *Class and Colour in South Africa: 1850–1950* (Cambridge, MA; International Defence and Aid Fund, 1983); Tom Lodge, *Black Politics in South Africa since 1945* (New York: Longman, 1983), and Nancy Clark and William H. Worger, *South Africa: The Rise and Fall of Apartheid* (Harlow: Pearson Longman, 2004). Also consulted were Robert Ross, *A Concise History of South Africa* (Cambridge, U.K.: Cambridge University Press, 1999) and Leonard Thompson, *A History of South Africa* (New Haven, Conn.: Yale University Press, 1990).

Especially valuable for its articles on political resistance in the 1960s was *The Road to Democracy in South Africa, Volume 1 (1960–1970)*, (Cape Town: Zebra Press, 2004 (South African Democracy Education Trust)). Individual essays used in this anthology were: Madeleine Fullard, 'State Repression in the 1960s', pp. 341–390; Martin Legassick and Chris Saunders, 'Aboveground Activity in the 1960s', pp. 661–689; Robin Kayser and M. Adhikari, 'Land and Liberty!: The African People's Democratic Union of Southern Africa during the 1960s', pp. 319–339; Bernard Magubane et al., 'The Turn to Armed Struggle', pp. 53–145; and Nhlanhla Ndebele and Noor Nieftagodien, 'The Morogoro Conference: A Moment of Self-reflection', pp. 573–599.

Nelson Mandela's *Long Walk to Freedom* (Boston: Little, Brown, 1994) was useful for political background as were the following autobiographies and biographies: Stephen Clingman, *Bram Fischer: Afrikaner Revolutionary* (Cape Town: David Philip, 1998); Ruth First, *117 Days: An Account of Confinement and Interrogation under the South*

African Ninety-Day Detention Law (London: Bloomsbury, 1988); Sadie Forman and André Odendaal (eds.), *Lionel Forman: A Trumpet from the Housetops* (Cape Town: David Philip, 1992); Ahmed Kathrada, *Memoirs* (Cape Town: Zebra Press, 2004); *Luthuli: Speeches of Chief Albert John Luthuli*, compiled by E.S. Reddy (Durban: Madiba Publishers, and Bellville: UWC Historical and Cultural Centre, 1991); Ismail Meer, *A Fortunate Man* (Cape Town: Zebra Press, 2002); Elinor Sisulu, *Walter and Albertina Sisulu: In Our Lifetime* (2nd edn) (Cape Town: David Philip, 2003); and Walter Sisulu (in conversation with George M. Houser and Herbert Shore), *I Will Go Singing: Walter Sisulu Speaks of his Life and the Struggle for Freedom in South Africa* (Robben Island Museum, n.d.). Biographical information on ANC activists was also found on two websites: www.sahistory.org.za and www.anc.org.za. Wikipedia also served as a source for biographies.

For the activities of the Special Branch in its surveillance, interrogation, and torture of individuals: *Truth and Reconciliation Commission of South Africa Report*, volumes 2–4, especially volume 3 (London: Macmillan, 1999).

Specific works on the South African Communist Party were Stephen Ellis and Tsepo Sechaba, *Comrades against Apartheid: The ANC and the South African Communist Party in Exile* (London: James Currey, 1992); Dominic Fortescue, 'The Communist Party of South Africa and the African Working Class in the 1940s', *International Journal of African Historical Studies* 24, 3 (1991), 481–512; and Eddy Maloka, *The South African Communist Party in Exile, 1963–1990* (Pretoria: Africa Institute of South Africa, 2002).

For the history and politics of nursing in South Africa: Blanche La Guma's own essays ('A Child Is Born', *New Age*, 2 August 1956; 'Nursing Apartheid Will Ruin a Noble Profession', *New Age* 20 June 1957, p. 6; and 'Nursing by Pigment', *Nursing News*, July 1957, pp. 32–33); and Shula Marks, *Divided Sisterhood: Race, Class, and Gender in the*

South African Nursing Profession (Basildon: Palgrave Macmillan, 1994). Also consulted was Alma Grobbelaar, 'South Africa Experiments with the Basic Collegiate Program', *American Journal of Nursing*, 58, 10 (October 1958), 1401–1402. Infant mortality rates were available in Harry T. Phillips, 'An Inter-Racial Study in Social Conditions and Infant Mortality in Cape Town', *Milbank Memorial Fund Quarterly* 35, 1 (January 1957), 7–28.

For the London years (1966–1978), the most useful work on IDAF (International Defence and Aide) was Denis Herbstein, *White Lies: Canon Collins and the Secret War against Apartheid* (Pretoria: Human Sciences Research Council, 2005). Also helpful was the Canon Collins Trust website: www.canoncollins.org.uk/about/aboutHistoryIDAF. shtml. The 1971 spy scandal between the Soviet Union and Great Britain was recorded by the *New York Times* in a series of articles in September 1971 written by Anthony Lewis, John M. Lee, and Benjamin Welles. Also consulted was Terry Bell and Dumisa Ntsebeza, *Unfinished Business: South Africa, Apartheid, and the Truth* (London: Verso, 2003).

For information on the World Peace Council and specifically Soviet activity on the World Peace Council: Jeffrey Richelson, *Sword and Shield: The Soviet Intelligence and Security Apparatus* (Cambridge, MA: Ballinger Publishing, 1986); Jeffrey Richelson, *A Century of Spies: Intelligence in the Twentieth Century* (Oxford: Oxford University Press, 1995); Christopher Andrew and Vasili Mitrokhin, *The Sword and the Shield: The Mitrokhin Archive and the Secret History of the KGB* (New York: Basic Books, 1999); Philip Agee, *Inside the Company, CIA Diary* (New York: Bantam, 1984); WPC, *Peace Courier*, 1989, no. 4; i-p-o.org/chandra.htm; and Wikipedia: 'World Peace Council'.